Lecture Notes in Artificial Intelligence   8757

Subseries of Lecture Notes in Computer Science

More information about this series at http://www.springer.com/series/1244

Ronald Böck · Francesca Bonin
Nick Campbell · Ronald Poppe (Eds.)

Multimodal Analyses enabling Artificial Agents in Human-Machine Interaction

Second International Workshop, MA3HMI 2014
Held in Conjunction with INTERSPEECH 2014
Singapore, Singapore, September 14, 2014
Revised Selected Papers

 Springer

Editors
Ronald Böck
Otto von Guericke University
Magdeburg
Germany

Francesca Bonin
Trinity College
Dublin
Ireland

Nick Campbell
Trinity College
Dublin
Ireland

Ronald Poppe
Utrecht University
Utrecht
The Netherlands

ISSN 0302-9743   ISSN 1611-3349   (electronic)
Lecture Notes in Artificial Intelligence
ISBN 978-3-319-15556-2   ISBN 978-3-319-15557-9   (eBook)
DOI 10.1007/978-3-319-15557-9

Library of Congress Control Number: 2015931916

LNCS Sublibrary: SL7 – Artificial Intelligence

Springer International Publishing AG Switzerland is part of Springer Science+Business Media
(www.springer.com)

Preface

The research in Human-Machine Interaction (HMI) is an emerging topic in various research communities. It is not only a matter in computer sciences but moreover, it is a subject of psychology, engineering, neuroscience, cognitive science, and many related disciplines. The connecting question for all the researchers in the above-mentioned communities is:

> How can the user's behavior be analyzed to improve the interaction between humans and machines?

For this, we usually investigate at first the interaction between humans to understand how the fragile interplay and interrelationship of communication partners is established and afterwards pursued. The complex scenario of a dialog between (even two) inter-locutors is enriched with subtle reactions and characteristics. Just for human observers, a correct judgement according to aspects like social context and background, emotions and feelings, possible reactions, is quite challenging. Fortunately, a human observer is able to incorporate a huge variety of multiple knowledge sources and multimodal sensor inputs. Such knowledge is, for instance, the contextual information of the current interaction, the social and cultural background of the communication partners, or the possible and intended goal of the discussion. On the other hand, sensory inputs like speech and sound, gaze, facial expression, gestures can be used to enhance and enable a detailed analysis of the interaction process.

In recent research activities, the aim is to transfer such considerations to HMI. Like a human observer, a machine should use as much information as possible to derive a correct judgement of an interaction. A multimodal investigation of the communication is, therefore, mandatory in order to understand valuable cues that have to be considered in the machine's internal situation evaluation. Such advice applies not only to the analysis part but also to the output or interface design. In general, a suitable interface will consider both input and output in an appropriate way. For this, one of the goals in building multimodal user interfaces is to make the interaction between user and system as natural as possible. Again, the most natural form of interaction is how humans interact with each other.

While the analysis of human-human communication and HMI has resulted in many insights and further, an increased understanding of interaction, transferring this knowledge to a real-time situation, is still challenging. To use technical systems in a proper way in daily interaction a real-time evaluation is necessary and important. It requires that input from a user, coming from speech, gaze, facial expression, and any other modality is recorded and interpreted in real-time or with minimal delay. The interpretation can be either semantic, or could aim at more affective properties such as the personality, mood, or intentions of the user. For this, the combined effort of multiple aforementioned disciplines have to be taken into account to achieve such a goal. Finally, a system or an agent also needs to respond appropriately to the user without delays to ensure that the interaction is smooth.

To establish systems or, in a sense of a more human-like interpretation, (artificial virtual) agents, we identify three main topics to be emphasized as important research areas.

Multimodal Annotation. The generation of agents and systems is based on data. In general, most communities prefer datasets that are already preprocessed and thus, suitable for direct development. On the other hand, this implies that the corpora contain significant material which will be usually explored and provided during annotation. In closed connection also issues of proper features to be applied in systems are important to discuss. Notice that such a processing of data is not only focused on annotation but covers all steps from data collection, (pre-)processing, annotation up to feature extraction and (sub-)symbolic interpretation of the given material. As we already discussed, a proper investigation of an interaction is mostly valuable in a multimodal fashion. Hence, existing approaches have to be adapted and – if necessary – enhanced to be feasible for further analyses. Currently, the idea of open data is an emerging topic and thus, should be linked towards multimodal data.

Multimodal Analyses. The analyses of data are complex. Each observed modality has its own characteristics which have to be considered in detail. For instance, from speech various aspects could be covered: the contextual information, the prosodic and para-linguistic features, and intentional cues. The same variety can be seen in video material where the analysis of several signals, such as eye gaze, gestures, postures, is a key element. Real-time processing of all this is the real challenge. In this context, questions of fusion as well as combination of features and results are discussed in recent research.

Applications and Systems. Finally, the achievements of analyses will result in systems and (artificial virtual) agents combining proper inputs and outputs to handle an inter-action in a human-like manner. The development of feasible applications is a crucial and challenging issue. For this, generally, user studies are conducted which are based on Wizard-of-Oz or mock-up scenarios. Nevertheless, such studies provide insights and understandings of theoretical and methodological approaches which can be directly transferred to setups of agents. Further, they usually lead to novel applications. Therefore, the development of systems and agents has to be fostered.

Based on these considerations and having in mind the challenges of current HMI and (artificial virtual) agents, we conceptualized the 2nd International Workshop on Multimodal Analyses enabling Artificial Agents in Human-Machine Interaction (MA3HMI). The workshop was held in conjunction with INTERSPEECH 2014, on September 14, 2014 in Singapore.

The MA3HMI workshop aimed to bring together researchers working on the analysis of multimodal recordings as a means to develop systems that can interact with humans. (Artificial) agents can be regarded in their broadest sense, including virtual chat agents, empathic speech interfaces, and life-style coaches on a smart phone. Complementary to the 2012 edition of MA3HMI, the focus of the 2014 MA3HMI was on speech which transfers both content and social information. We were particularly interested in speech technologies for HMI, and the combination of speech and natural language processing with the analysis of other modalities.

We encouraged researchers to present and discuss their papers that concern the different development phases of HMI, including the recording and online analysis of multimodal conversations, the modeling of the dialog, and the user evaluation of such systems. Further, tools and systems that address real-time conversations with (artificial virtual) agents were also within the topics of MA3HMI.

From the submitted contributions, which received at least two independent reviews, nine papers were selected for oral presentation and publication in this issue of Lecture Notes on Artificial Intelligence (LNAI). The papers were grouped in the sections "Human-Machine Interaction" and "Dialogs and Speech Recognition" which serve also as main parts of this book.

In addition to the oral presentations, we had a lively and really interesting plenary discussion on hot topics in the context of HMI and agents. We thank all authors and participants of the MA3HMI workshop for their contribution.

Furthermore, the workshop was enriched by an extraordinary keynote talk given by Prof. Nick Campbell, Speech Communication Lab at Trinity College Dublin. In his plenary talk Prof. Campbell presented a novel corpus for multimodal studies of interactions. Further, he provided insights into the data generation and processing of such multimodal datasets. Moreover, Nick Campbell shared his ideas and thoughts on analyses and what to do and where to go in the research of HMI. We thank Prof. Nick Campbell for accepting our invitation for a keynote talk, his contribution, and the subsequent discussion.

Further, we thank the members of the Program Committee for their effort in reviewing the submissions and identifying the most relevant papers for the year 2014 MA3HMI.

Our sincere gratitude goes also to Springer and to Alfred Hofmann and Anna Kramer as well as their team for their continuous support and all the effort in preparing the current issue of LNAI.

We thank the INTERSPEECH 2014 workshops chair, Chai Wutiwiwatchai, and the local arrangement team for their support. Without their help the workshop's venue would not have been so well prepared. Further, we also acknowledge Singapore Expo and their collaborators for hosting the workshop.

Finally, our gratitude goes to our generous sponsors, the Transregional Collaborative Research Center "Companion Technology" and the FastNet project, which provided financial support for MA3HMI. Further, we acknowledge the endorsement of ISCA.

October 2014   Ronald Böck
                                                           Francesca Bonin
                                                            Nick Campbell
                                                            Ronald Poppe

Organization

Organizing Committee

Ronald Böck	Otto von Guericke University Magdeburg, Germany
Francesca Bonin	Trinity College Dublin, Ireland
Nick Campbell	Trinity College Dublin, Ireland
Ronald Poppe	Utrecht University, The Netherlands

Invited Speaker

Nick Campbell	Trinity College Dublin, Ireland

Program Committee

Xavier Anguera Miro	Telefonica Research, Spain
Christian Becker-Asano	University Freiburg, Germany
Roman Bednarik	University of Eastern Finland, Finland
Nick Campbell	Trinity College Dublin, Ireland
Laurence Devillers	University of Paris-Sorbonne 4, France
Wentao Gu	The University of Tokyo, Japan
Zakia Hammal	Carnegie Mellon University, USA
Dirk Heylen	University of Twente, The Netherlands
Kristiina Joniken	University of Helsinki, Finland
Stefan Kopp	Bielefeld University, Germany
Satoshi Nakamura	Nara Institute of Science and Technology, Japan
Dietmar Rösner	Otto von Guericke University Magdeburg, Germany
Jose San Pedro Wandelmer	Telefonica Research, Spain
Stefan Scherer	University of Southern California, USA
Björn Schuller	Imperial College London, UK
Merlin Teodosia Suarez	De La Salle University, Philippines
Jianhua Tao	Chinese Academy of Sciences, China
Jürgen Trouvain	Saarland University, Germany
Alessandro Vinciarelli	University of Glasgow, UK
Carl Vogel	Trinity College Dublin, Ireland
Andreas Wendemuth	Otto von Guericke University Magdeburg, Germany

Sponsors

CRC "Companion Technology"

sfb transregio 62
Companion Technology

FastNet

FastNet

Contents

Keynote

Annotating the TCD D-ANS Corpus – A Multimodal Multimedia Monolingual Biometric Corpus of Spoken Social Interaction

Nick Campbell[1](✉) and Shannon Hennig[2]

[1] Speech Communication Lab, Trinity College Dublin, Dublin, Ireland
nick@tcd.ie
[2] Inclusive Communication Ltd., Wellington, New Zealand
shannon@inclusive-communication.co.nz

Abstract. This paper describes a recently created multimodal biometric corpus of spontaneous casual spoken interaction recorded at Trinity College Dublin, the University of Dublin, in Ireland, and currently being made available for wider dissemination. The paper focusses on the use of this corpus for training or learning about the needs and limitations of an interactive spoken dialogue interface for human-machine communication. Since the corpus is still very new and only recently released, the paper does not present research findings based on an analysis of the content but instead suggests methods and goals for annotating the material so that future researchers can use it to design more sensitive interfaces for speech synthesis in spoken dialogue systems. The paper is an extended version of an invited talk at the MA3HMI workshop.

Keywords: Spoken dialogue · Multimodal interaction · Biometric data · Capture & analysis · Interactive speech synthesis · Perceptual computing

1 Introduction

Human-computer interfaces for the general public are not new but they are rapidly becoming a key technology, as computing devices become smaller and more ubiquitous. Wearable or pocketable computers are now common, and the range of sensors they incorporate is growing at a rate we could not have predicted ten years ago.

Speech-based interaction with machines or knowledge-systems is no longer a dream but is now an everyday reality as the world of digital information is opening up to people-in-the-street, with young children now being exposed to smart devices with swipable and voice-activated interfaces perhaps even before they learn to use a pencil or pen.

'Perceptual computing' might now be a brand-name (of Intel) but it reflects the way that machines are becoming sensitive to humans in a more human-like way; incorporating gesture, tone-of-voice, speech and facial dynamics, and near-field interaction modalities as part of the basic operating system of a modern-day tablet or personal computer to enable new modes of interaction between people and machines (see Fig. 1).

© Springer International Publishing Switzerland 2015
R. Böck et al. (Eds.): MA3HMI 2014 Workshop, LNAI 8757, pp. 3–12, 2015.
DOI: 10.1007/978-3-319-15557-9_1

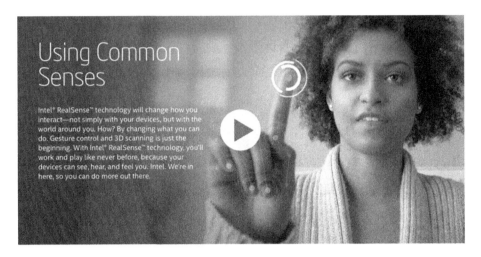

Fig. 1. From a recent Intel advert for Perceptual Computing. Note that the computer is aware of the shape of the hand (and probably facial expression) as well as being capable of speech and gesture processing

This technology which is with us now, will depend heavily on advances in natural-language processing and virtual-agent rendering to facilitate the natural forms of spoken interaction that are so characteristic of human social interaction. Devices will have to learn to read the signals that we commonly use to punctuate and inform our speech, and to 'read between the lines' of physical utterances and gestures to be able to infer the cognitive states and intentions that underly them.

It is therefore even more necessary that we should have a complete understanding of these processes so that advances can be made in the soft side of the technology to keep up with the rapid advances in computer hardware and memory capabilities. This inspired us to collect a corpus of normal everyday spoken interaction with not just audio and video recordings but also biometric sensors to provide a possibly more objective measure of the participant states and interactions in the course of a conversation. From this corpus we hope to learn how people signal their role(s) in a conversation so that computer interfaces might be better able to read those signals and act on them without the need for explicit commands.

The following sections briefly provide some background to the TCD D-ANS corpus [1], and mention some technological issues related to speech processing in human-computer interfaces before discussing the annotation requirements of the new corpus.

2   Serendipitous Liaisons

When Shannon Hennig came to visit our lab in November 2011, she brought with her a paper by Beukelman [2] of Nebraska whose analogy of 'right hand'

and 'left hand' messages (referring to the melody and harmony parts on a piano but with clear implications to human speech) seemed closely related to much of what we had discussed in earlier meetings about the different modes of speech activity in social contexts. It became the seed of an idea by which we determined to obtain measures of bilateral neural activity and learn something of its relation to task-based and chat-based, or formal and social modes of interaction in casual conversational speech.

Her interest at that time was in the candidacy of physiological measurements for implicit control of emotional speech synthesis. My earlier work on the development of expressive speech synthesis overlapped well with her ideas of morphological computation in natural speech (inspired by Pfeifer, Bongard and Grand, 2007 p. 96 [3]) whereby environmental triggers initiate Autonomous Nervous System (ANS) activity which results in physiological body changes such that vocal-tract constriction (for example) influences voice quality, inducing subtle changes in the quality of the speech signal that can be picked up by the listener who then infers para-linguistic or extra-linguistic information from that aspect of the signal in order to better parse the utterance in context.

We wanted to know if there are correlations between variations in physiological measures and vocal acoustic measures that we could use in (either or both) processing the input signal from humans engaging in conversation, and generating an equivalent signal rich in paralinguistic information for the synthesis of more natural-sounding machine-generated speech. Her then recent work with Autonomic Nervous System responses (measured using Affectiva's Q-Sensors [4]) in relation to stressful speaking situations convinced us that there was value in measuring and learning from similar responses in more casual informal social speech.

As detailed in [1], Q-sensors measure Electrodermal Activity (EDA, also known as galvanic skin response and skin conductance) which is how readily a small current of electricity passes across the skin. EDA is associated with activation of the sympathetic branch of the ANS and is correlated with increases in physiological arousal [5] Change in EDA is associated with changes in attention, perception, problem-solving, movement, and emotion [5,6].

3   Recording Setup

The Speech Communication Lab in the Centre for Language and Communication Studies at Trinity College Dublin has excellent facilities for multimodal recording of casual spoken interactions, both human-human and human-machine, so after the purchase of some extra Q-sensors, we were able to start recording with the help of friends and colleagues.

Consent forms were prepared and subjects informed of their rights to withdraw at any time, as well as being warned not to broach any particularly sensitive topics as their conversations were being recorded. All participants were familiar with the surroundings and equipment in the lab so none were in any way intimidated by being seated in the midst of microphones and cameras, though none except Shannon had any experience of wearing the wrist-watch-like Q-sensors.

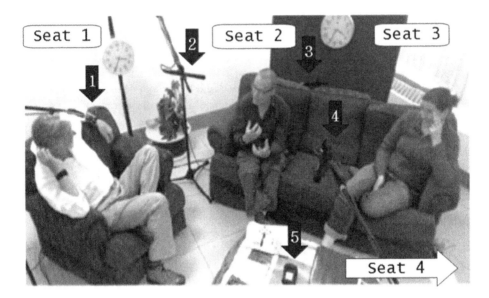

Fig. 2. A scene from the D-ANS corpus (overhead webcam view) showing seating and microphone placement. Participants each wearing two Q-sensors

The first day of recordings was very much one of experiment. We needed to find ways to effectively and efficiently link a set of videos of people talking (and gesturing and moving about) with the accelometer data from their wrists during these videos. We needed to find optimal positions for camera placement and to find locations for microphones that would be able to pick-up fine vocal fluctuations while not being invasive or hampering the free movement of the speakers in any way.

We also discussed strategy and planned ways of maximising the variety of participants' speaking styles across various dimensions of formality, familiarity, and conviviality. The recordings from Day-1 are not part of the publicly-available corpus but do provide useful baseline measures from which we can compare the performance of the same subjects in the later recordings. They can however be made available to interested researchers upon request.

Figure 2 (from [1]) shows the layout of the studio corner where the recordings were made. Shannon is on the right and the first author on the left, with a colleague and friend from another Irish university in the middle. Participants were free to move around, and change seats. The relaxed atmosphere of the recordings can perhaps be seen from the poses of the participants. Freshly signed consent forms are visible on the table.

There are microphones in abundance, and cameras recording from several angles, but none of the equipment is intrusive in any physical way. Two clocks (radio syncronised) ensure that the output of all cameras can be roughly aligned. Shotgun microphones provide the main audio recordings but these are backed up by high-quality far-field microphones and a small portable stereo desktop

Fig. 3. A scene from the D-ANS corpus showing the different camera views.

recorder for simple fast navigation and backup. Lower-quality audio from the video cameras themselves can be used for accurate alignment of the videos.

Figure 3 shows a scene from Day-2 with the overview webcam display at the top and two high-definition video images from each of the working cameras below. The webcam, like the table-top Roland Edirol audio recorder, is primarily for backup and general overview processing for humans; the working cameras and the Sennheiser microphones are for more detailed machine-processing of the interactions. In these images the Q-sensor ANS recorders are visible on each wrist of all participants. We recorded bilateral signals so that later analyses would be able to test for any effect of hemispheric laterality.

4   The Machine's Task

This section discusses some predictable advances in speech-processing technology that might be of use in future Perceptual Computing. In particular it proposes ways to overcome some limitations in automatic speech recognition, and suggests some improvements that might help to make speech synthesis more interactive.

In a simplified world, a speech synthesiser just has to make an appropriate sequence of speech-like sounds and the user *(horrible word)* or customer *(even worse)* is expected to understand and perhaps act on the linguistic content of the speech. In the real world however, most speech synthesisers don't even know whether or not there is a listener present! No normal human would start speaking in such a context[1] (unless speaking to oneself, when a listener is either not needed or present by default). The first task of our sentient synthesiser in an ideal human-computer speech-based interface would therefore be to check whether or not speech might be appropriate at any given moment. Perhaps the only thing worse for a synthesiser than speaking into a void is speaking out when silence is preferred, thereby interrupting a human conversation or auditory performance.

Most human speakers will also check that their message is getting across. This does not happen with the typical speech synthesiser of today. People are just expected to understand. A careful synthesiser might even check whether the listener, if present, can actually understand the language being used - the machine might be capable of rendering perfect Chinese, for example, but if the listener is not familiar with that language, then any linguistic utterance generated will effectively be meaningless. There are of course many non-linguistic utterances that are common across many pairs of human languages, but few synthesisers are capable of rendering them appropriately.

So the first five checks that our sentient speech synthesiser should make are, in order: (a) is there a human present and a need to speak?; (b) does that person qualify as a listener (i.e., close enough, with working ears, etc.)?; (c) is the person capable of hearing the sound?; (d) is the person attending to the sound?; and finally, (e) is the function of the sound being appreciated or understood? (which is approaching a philosophical distinction but can be approximately estimated from the synchrony of behavioural responses). If all five conditions are satisfied to a certain level of probability, then the higher-level dialogue component of this speech-based interface can start to estimate whether there is rapport reached between the speaker and listener, or whether a repair is necessary, perhaps some rephrasing of the speech at a different level or genre so that satisfactory comprehension can be achieved.

The above are measures of 'engagement'. In the context of a spoken dialogue, engagement is a feature of cognitive attentional states. Clearly the speaker is engaged; this can often be simply measured by a correlation of mouth movement and presence of speech-like sound. We do not have to pay attention to the content of the speech to know that a person is speaking, and by definition therefore, engaged in that speech.

In Fig. 2 it is perhaps the person in the centre who is speaking. How can we know this, or how would a sensitive machine be able to estimate such information? Perhaps from the shape of the hands. Even in this still image, it is apparent that his hand gesture is supporting a spoken utterance. The person might actually be holding a black bottle, though this interpretation is less likely. But how do we estimate or infer the listeners' cognitive engagement or attentional state? Simply being physically present is not enough. Some difference between hearing and listening must be inferred.

---

[1] Broadcasters or actors might be an exception to this general rule.

In Fig. 2, both Shannon and Nick appear to be striking a 'listening' pose. They are facing the speaker and have hands either resting or close to an ear. From this still image, we as humans can process much of the visual information and make inferences from these clues about the attentional states of the three people present. It should not be difficult for a synthesiser (or its sensing component) to do the same. If the image is moving, as in a video, then use can be made of coverbal synchrony [7] as the listeners' heads, and parts of their bodies, should be moving in some way that links to the timing patterns and phrasing of the speech.

Laughter can also be a clear indicator of engagement and confirms (if appropriately timed) that the listener is probably paying attention. Nodding, co-gesturing, offering backchannel utterances, interrupting appropriately, etc., can all indicate some degree of engagement in a conversation. So the synthesiser needs to have eyes and ears as well as a 'mouth', but a clever speech recogniser will also be able to make use of these multimodal cues to infer meaning when the actual sound may be too ambiguous to translate[2].

Life will not be easy for our sentient synthesiser; particularly as there may be more than one person present on the scene, and in that case the speaker (in this case a machine) may have to compete with other participants for the right to speak. Some awareness of the cognitive states of the participants will be a necessary part of that dialogue process.

5   The Corpus Annotation Goal

The first use to which we are putting the D-ANS Corpus is for the development of advanced dialogue interface technology. The Q-sensor-derived biometric measures, even at a simple glance, confirm that they can provide useful information for confirming the automatic inference of engagement as estimated from audio and video signals and through use of measures of coverbal synchrony.

Figure 4 shows electrodermal activity (EDA) measures for three people (both wrists) for Day-3 of the recordings. The small grey area near the centre represents one five-minute section of that measure which is shown in more detail for one speaker in Fig. 5. The latter figure shows vertical bars representing speech from each participant (blue for the speaker whose EDA plot is shown above). There is a clear relation between onset of speech and an increase in measured activity. Further relations between the timing of the EDA changes and activity of other speakers is currently being explored in a more systematic way.

We employ statistical means to test these correlations and machine-learning to test the degreee to which audio-visual information can be used as a predictor of the ANS responses as indicated by the EDA signal. To better validate these techniques we also need human-generated annotations of events in the discourse, but this is an expensive and time-consuming task.

---

[2] Think of the various ways of saying the word 'yes' for example, and the wide range of different meanings they represent!

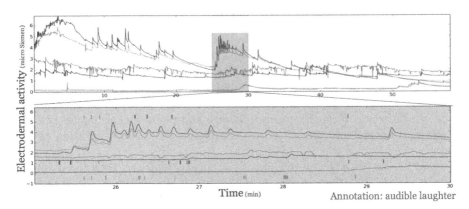

Fig. 4. Data from Day-3 showing electrodermal activity from both wrists of the three participants. The small grey box at the centre-top marks a five-minute section that is shown in more detail in the following figure

Since laughter is such a common feature of casual speech, it is also the first feature that we annotate. The text of each utterance, however, is of lesser importance. It is not really necessary to know the full details of the linguistic content when it is the functional effect of each utterance that most interests us. The social dynamics of a conversation can be equivalent whether the topic of discussion is 'pasta' or 'car engines'; it is the dynamics of turn-taking, and the group involvement that is of most interest to us here, and a simple voice-activity detector (VAD) in conjunction with image processing can provide almost as much information as a full manual transcription in this case. The nature of turn-taking and the length of each utterance can be easily calculated from VAD data which is both visually appealing and machine-friendly for processing. It is also helpful to privacy not to have to reveal too many details of the actual conversations when discoursal dynamics, or conversational metadata, may be sufficient.

The correlations seen in Fig. 5 can be readily detected by automatic processing. The value or meaning of these correlations, however, is what we most need to determine at the present time, and that can only be achieved by human intervention. Our human annotators can determine the tone of the laughter much better than any automatic detector is yet able to; positive supporting laughter, or humorous outbursts contrast with embarrassed or hesitant laughter which might indicate a social negative state.

6   Sharing

The corpus is being made available to interested researchers under the following web-page: http://www.speech-data.jp/nick/d-ans/.

The participants have agreed to share this data with the research community, provided that the details of the personal stories and identifying information

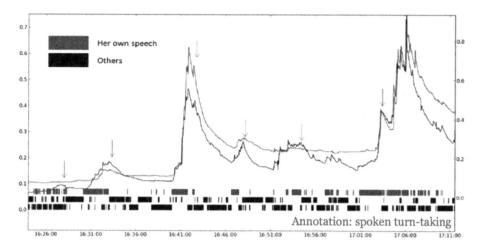

Fig. 5. Five minutes of EDA activity, aligned with speech activity, showing clear spikes coinciding with onset of her speech and turn-taking

(i.e., names, birth dates, etc.) caught on camera not be shared in any resulting publications or presentations and in general be treated as confidential.

As this is currently active work in progress, the state of the pages is liable to change at short notice, but we invite collaborative study of this material and offer it under a Creative Commons Attribution-NonCommercial International license. The annotations, media, and biosignal data will be shared on the website along with sample video clips to allow any interested parties to have a sense of the type of interaction captured in this corpus. The full corpus (3–5 audio files, 3 video files, biosignal csv file for each day of recording) will be made available for noncommercial research purposes to any interested researchers upon the return of signed release forms found on the website.

7 Summary and Conclusion

This paper is an updated version of an invited talk presented by the first author at the MA3HMI international workshop in Singapore, which brought together researchers working on the analysis of multimodal recordings as a means to develop systems that can interact with humans. The core of the oral presentation was to describe the corpus as originally presented at LREC 2014 [1]. The present paper gives more of the background to the development of the corpus and of the intended uses to which it will be put in our work at the Speech Communication Lab in Dublin and at NAIST in Japan. I am grateful to the organisers of the workshop for giving me the opportunity to discuss these ideas and to Shannon for joining me in the written version of the paper.

We welcome interest in the corpus and are happy to share it within the research community. Collaborative work opens up greater opportunities for further research and the technology is still at a pre-competitive stage where most benefit can be gained through a sharing of the tasks. It can be commercialised at a later stage when greater understanding of the potentials and limitations of each approach has been achieved.

Acknowledgements. This work was carried out in the Speech Communication Lab at Trinity College Dublin and was supported by the SFI FastNet (project 09/IN.1/1263). The corpus collection was conducted as part of Shannon's doctoral work, which was funded by Universita degli Studi di Genova and the Instituto Italiano di Tecnologia. The work was co-funded as part of the Japanese Government KAKEN research into MOSAIC: "Models of Spontaneous and Interactive Communication" We are grateful to Fred Cummins and Brian Vaughan and thankful for the annotation efforts of Emer Gilmartin and Celine De Looze.

References

1. Hennig, S., Chellali, R., Campbell, N.: The D-ANS corpus: the Dublin-Autonomous Nervous System corpus of biosignal and multimodal recordings of conversational speech. In: Proceedings of the ELRA, the 9th Edition of the Language Resources and Evaluation Conference. Reykjavik, Iceland, pp. 26–31 (2014)
2. Beukelman, D.R.: There are some things you just can't say with your right hand. Augmented and Assistive Communication (1989)
3. Pfeifer, R., Bongard, J., Grand, S.: How the Body Shapes the Way We Think: A New View of Intelligence. MIT Press, Cambridge (2007)
4. Affectiva Q-sensors. http://qsensor-support.affectiva.com
5. Dawson, M.E., Schell, A.M., Dilion, D.L.: The electrodermal system. In: Cacioppo, J.T., Tassinary, L.G., Berntson, G.G. (eds.) Handbook of Psychophysiology, pp. 159–181. Cambridge University Press, New York (2007)
6. Calvo, R.A., D'Mello, S.: Affect detection: an interdisciplinary review of models, methods, and their applications. IEEE Trans. Affect. Comput. **1**(1), 18–37 (2010)
7. Rojc, M., Campbell, N.: Coverbal Synchrony in Human-Machine Interaction. CRC Press, Boca Raton (2013)

Human-Machine Interaction

Steps Towards More Natural Human-Machine Interaction via Audio-Visual Word Prominence Detection

Martin Heckmann[(⊠)]

Honda Research Institute Europe GmbH, 63073 Offenbach/Main, Germany
martin.heckmann@honda-ri.de

Abstract. We investigate how word prominence can be detected from the acoustic signal and movements of the speaker's head and mouth. Our research is based on a corpus with 12 English speakers which contains in addition to the speech signal also videos of the talker's head. To extract the word prominence information we use on one hand functionals calculated on the features and on the other hand Functional PCA (FPCA) to extract information from the contours. Combining the functionals and the contour information we obtain a discrimination accuracy between prominent and non-prominent words of 81 %. We show in particular that the visual channel is very informative for some speakers. Furthermore, we also introduce a system which extracts the prominence information online while a user is interacting with the system. The online system only uses acoustic information.

Keywords: Audio-visual · Prominence · Contour · FPCA · Online

1 Introduction

Spoken language is much more than the words we say. It comprises also information on the speaker's traits and states as personality and emotional state [9,36,37]. A truly natural interaction with an artificial agent, be it a virtual agent or a robot, requires that the agent is able to recognize and synthesize all of these aspects of human communication. Many efforts have been done to equip agents with the abilities to infer and produce different affective states [8,35]. In addition to its affective dimension the prosody of a sentence modulates its meaning (e. g. from a statement to a question) or the relevance the different words have for the speaker in the utterance (e. g. wide vs. narrow focus). The necessity of incorporating these dimensions in the speech synthesis process has well been accepted. Yet on the analysis side much less effort has been spent, in particular when looking on the multimodal aspects of prosody. Words which are strongly emphasized by the speaker and hence are perceived as very prominent by the listener frequently indicate a correction after a misunderstanding [41]. Endowing a machine with the capabilities to use this information is the target of our and previous research [26,27]. These words are also visually prominent, i. e. when

© Springer International Publishing Switzerland 2015
R. Böck et al. (Eds.): MA3HMI 2014 Workshop, LNAI 8757, pp. 15–24, 2015.
DOI: 10.1007/978-3-319-15557-9_2

only observing and not acoutically listening to the speaker [2,5,16,29,40]. Previously algorithms have been developed to detect these prominent words from the acoustic signal [26,27,33]. In [17] we presented an approach which also integrates information on the speaker's head and mouth movement to detect prominent words. In this paper we extend our approach on one hand by including a model for the representation of prosodic contours over time, namely Functional Principal Component Analysis (FPCA). On the other hand we also present an online system which is able to detect the prominent words in a real-time interaction with the user. For the moment the online system only relies on the acoustic channel.

In the next section we introduce the dataset we used for our experiments and training of the online system. We describe the different features extracted from the acoustic and visual channel and in particular the contour modeling in Sect. 3 Following this Sect. 4 will present the results of the classification experiments and Sect. 5 will discuss them. After that we will introduce the online system in Sect. 6. Then we will give a conclusion in Sect. 7.

2   Dataset

Our target scenario is the detection of corrected words via prosodic cues while a human is interacting with an agent. To simulate this we recorded subjects interacting via speech in a Wizard of Oz experiment with a computer in a small game where they moved tiles to uncover a cartoon [17]. This game yielded utterances of the form 'place green in B one'. Occasionally, a misunderstanding of one word of the sequence was triggered and the corresponding word highlighted, verbally and visually. The subjects were told to repeat in these cases the phrase as they would do with a human, i.e. emphasizing the previously misunderstood word. However, they were not allowed to deviate from the sentence grammar by e.g. beginning with 'No'. This was expected to create a narrow focus condition (in contrast to the broad focus condition of the original utterance) and thereby making the corrected word highly prominent. The system interacted with the user via verbal feedback using the FESTIVAL speech synthesis system [6], pictures of a cartoon robot performing certain gestures, and visually highlighting different parts of the game. In total 16 native English speaking subjects were recorded [18]. The audio signal was originally sampled at 48 kHz and later downsampled to 16 kHz. For the video images a CCD camera with a resolution of 1280×1024 pixel and a frame rate of 25 Hz was used.

We trained HTK [43] on the Grid Corpus [12] followed by a speaker adaptation with a Maximum Likelihood Linear Regression (MLLR) step with a subsequent Maximum A-Posteriori (MAP) step to perform a forced alignment of the data. This forced alignment provides a temporal annotation of the data and is used in the following to determine the boundaries of the different words. Thereby we used a combination of RASTA-PLP and spectro-temporal HIST features [19] as this gave upon visual inspection better results than either of the feature sets alone or MFCC features.

Three human annotators annotated the recorded data with 4 levels of prominence for each word. We calculated the inter-annotator agreement with Fleiss' kappa κ. While doing so we binarized the annotations, i.e. only differentiating between prominent and non-prominent. We tested different binarizations and used the one where the agreement between all annotators was highest. Next, we calculated κ for each speaker individually. We then discarded all speakers where κ for the optimal binary annotation was below 0.5 ($0.4 < \kappa \leq 0.6$ is usually considered as moderate agreement). We have chosen such a rather low threshold to retain as many speakers as possible. This yields 12 speakers, 6 females and 6 males. For further processing those turns where the original utterance and a correction were available were selected. Overall we have 2023 turn pairs (original utterance + correction), i.e. on average $\approx$160 turn pairs per speaker. From these the word which was emphasized in the correction was determined. Then it was extracted as well in the original utterance as in the correction. This yields a dataset with each individual word taken from a broad and a narrow focus condition.

3 Features

We extracted different features from the acoustic and visual channel to capture the prosodic variations.

3.1 Acoustic Features

Since we expected the loudness l to better capture the perceptual correlates of prominence than the energy, we extracted it by filtering the signal with an 11th order IIR filter as described in [1], followed by the calculation of the instantaneous energy, smoothing with a low pass filter with a cut-off frequency of 10 Hz, and conversion into dB. Furthermore, we calculated D, the duration of the word and the gaps before and after the word as determined from the forced alignment. We also extracted the fundamental frequency f_0 (following [21]), interpolated values in the unvoiced regions via cubic splines and converted the results to semitones. To detect voicing we used an extension of the algorithm described in [24]. Finally, we also determined the spectral emphasis SE, i.e. the difference between the overall signal energy and the energy in a dynamically low-pass-filtered signal with a cut-off frequency of $1.5f_0$ [22].

3.2 Visual Features

To extract features from the visual channel we used the OpenCV library [7]. By its help we detected the nose in each image. Based on this we developed a tracking algorithm which yields the nose position over time. The nose does not move much during articulation relative to the head and is hence well suited to measure the rigid head movements. Starting from the nose we can determine the mouth region in the image via a fixed speaker independent offset from the nose. On each subsampled mouth image of size 100×100 pixels we calculated a two-dimensional Discrete Cosine Transform (DCT). Out of the 10000 coefficients per image we selected the 20 with the lowest spatial frequencies.

3.3 Functionals

Functionals are commonly extracted from the (acoustic) features to detect prominent words [26,27,33] or perform prosodic analysis in general [15]. We extracted the mean, max, min, spread (max-min) and variance along the word. Hereby word boundaries were determined by the forced alignment. Prior to the calcualtion of the functionals and the contour modeling detailed in the next section we normalized the prosodic features by their utterance mean and calculated their first and second derivative (except for duration).

3.4 Contour Modeling via Functional Principal Component Analyis

To capture all the information in the feature and to be more tolerant against noise a more holistic representation than functionals based on contours is promising. Different approaches have been proposed to exploit this contour information as e. g. the extraction of plateaus [42], approximation with Legendre polynomials [23], stylizations of pitch contours with line segments [38], the calculation of the DCT from the contour [15] and in [18] we proposed to use a probabilistic parabola fitting to the contour. Very recently the Functional Principal Component Analysis (FPCA) has been proposed to discriminate emotional from neutral speech [4]. As the results obtained by the FPCA looked promising we opted to also apply it to the task of word prominence detection.

Functional data analysis is a branch of statistics which operates on curves or functions instead to data points [3,28,32]. The first step in FPCA is the smoothing of the data. This transforms discrete-time contour data defined only for $n = 1 \ldots N$ to functions which are defined for all time instances t:

$$x^*(t) = \sum_{k=1}^{K} c_k \xi_k(t) \,, \tag{1}$$

where the ξ_k are the new base functions and the coefficients c_k determine their weight. By choosing the number of bases K one can obtain a trade-off between smoothing of undesired fluctuations and retaining fine details. The coefficients c_k are determined in a minimum error sense. The calculation is controlled by a penalty parameter λ balancing fitting error and roughness of the curve. Similar to standard PCA, in the next step we calculate a new orthonormal basis $\varphi(t)$ using PCA in the functions domain. Assuming zero mean for $x^*(t)$ the projections of the smoothed input segment $x^*(t)$ onto this new basis, also termed Principal Components, is:

$$y_u = \int \varphi_u(t) \, x^*(t) dt. \tag{2}$$

Table 1. Unweighted accuracies in % averaged over all 12 speakers. See the text for the meaning of the feature name and modeling abbreviations. A+V represents audio and video features combined. The asterisk indicates values which are statistically significantly better than using the functionals only for the given feature combination ($\alpha = 5\,\%$).

	l	f_0	Nose	DCT	Audio	Video	A+V
Functionals	71.6	76.1	67.1	69.4	79.0	69.7	79.3
FPCA	71.6	76.6	67.0	68.4	79.7	71.2	78.9
Functionals+FPCA	72.8*	77.8*	67.7	70.2	80.7*	71.2*	80.4*

The function $x^*(t)$ is then reconstructed using the U basis functions:

$$\hat{x}^*(t) = \sum_{u=1}^{U} y_u \varphi_u(t). \tag{3}$$

We retain the projections y_u as coefficients describing the contour segment. To calculate the FPCA we first linearly interpolated all segments on an equally spaced grid using B-splines. Due to the different feature rates in the acoustic (100 Hz) and visual (25 Hz) channel we used 30 and 10 points respectively. All steps for the FPCA were performed with the Matlab toolbox retrieved from [31]. We retained 10 coefficients for each dimension for the acoustic features and 7 for the visual ones along the time axis. The transformations were learned using all the data of one speaker.

4   Results

To discriminate prominent from non-prominent words we used a Support Vector Machine (SVM) with a Radial Basis Function Kernel implemented in LibSVM [11]. For each feature combination a grid search for C, the penalty parameter of the error term, and γ, the variance scaling factor of the basis function, was performed using the whole dataset. Prior to the grid search the data was normalized to the range $[-1\ldots1]$. With the found optimal parameters we trained an SVM on 75 % of the data and tested on the remaining 25 %. Hereby a 30 fold cross validation in which the data set was always split such that an identical number of elements is taken from both classes was run. To establish the 30 sets a sampling with replacement strategy was applied. This process was performed individually for each speaker.

As features we investigated loudness (l), f_0, the 2D nose position, the DCT calculated from the mouth region, the combination of all acoustic features, i. e. l, f_0, SE and duration, the combination of all visual features, i. e. nose and mouth DCT, and the combination of the acoustic and visual features. Table 1 shows the results averaged over all 12 speakers. For each of these feature sets we calculated

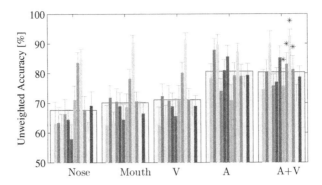

Fig. 1. Unweighted accuracies for different feature combinations (A represents results obtained from audio only, V from video only and A+V from the combination of audio and video). Each colored line indicates results for an individual speaker. The thin horizontal line on top visualizes the variance of the 30-fold cross-validation. An asterisk indicates a statistically significantly better result of the combination of A+V compared to A alone ($\alpha = 5\%$). The thick grey bar in the background depicts the mean over all speakers (Color figure online).

the unweighted accuracy when using only the functionals, the FPCA contour models or a combination of both.

As can be seen from Table 1 f_0 is clearly the strongest feature. The loudness l also performs quite well. For all feature sets the combination of the FPCA contour models with the funtionals yields equal or better results than either one alone. Cases where the difference is statistically significant are highlighted with an asterisk in Table 1.

In Fig. 1 results when using funtionals and FPCA are detailed for each speaker. As can be seen the nose and mouth DCT features perform well above chance level for all speakers. Figure 1 further shows that despite the decrease in performance on average when combining visual and acoustic features there is a strong gain from the visual features for some speakers.

5   Discussion

The results showed that the inclusion of prosodic contour models calculated via FPCA is in general beneficial for the detection of word prominence. They show in particular that not only the f_0 and energy contours carry important information but also the nose, resp. the head, movements and the evolution of the DCT coefficients calculated from the mouth region over time. As best results when looking on head movements (i. e. nose) only we obtain 67.7 % correct. When considering only the mouth movements (i. e. mouth DCT) we obtain 70.2 %. The best score we see when combining all visual features is 71.2 %. This is similar to the individual acoustic features but clearly inferior to the combination of all acoustic features. The overall best result we obtain with 80.7 % uses a combination of functionals and FPCA contour models of the acoustic features. A more detailed analysis of the visual and audio-visual results revealed that there is a large variation from speaker to speaker. These variations seem to be very individual as we found in [18] that a grouping of the speakers based on the accuracies obtained with the different acoustic features (e. g. fundamental frequency, energy or duration) did not yield consistent groups. With the current data we see most notably that for some speakers the visual channel improves results yet for others it deteriorates them. The nose movement yields for all speakers accuracies well above chance level (57.9 % for the worst speaker and 67.7 % on average). For two speakers we see more than 80 % correct when looking on the nose movements only. It has previously been shown that the nose, resp. rigid head, movement differs between prominent and non-prominent words, even though there was no consensus if this is the case for all speakers [13,14,16]. In our previous work on the same dataset we also only saw accuarcies above chance level for some speakers [18]. Yet due to the improved visual feature extraction we now see it for all speakers and in particular are able to quantify the information content via our recognition experiments, at least to some extend. When we combine the nose movements with the mouth features we obtain 91.5 % correct for one individual speaker. This is also the one speaker where we observe very significant improvements from the combination of the acoustic and visual channel (87.4 % vs. 92.6 %). In total we see similar improvements from the combination of visual and acoustic features for 4 speakers. However, averaged over all speakers results are inferior to using the acoustic features alone. We think that with further improvements on the extraction of the visual features they will show beneficial in general when combined with acoustic features.

6   Online System

It is well known that users change their speaking style when talking to a machine as compared to when talking to a human [39]. Whereas they usually use a rich intonation when they talk to humans, they talk with a rather flat and monotonous voice to a machine. Currently we are integrating the different aspects we presented above in an online system. Such an online integration will allow us to investigate how users adapt to a system which is sensitive to prosodic variations. They might adapt to a speaking style as they would apply when talking to a human. Yet they might as well adapt to an exaggerated style which can better be decoded by a machine able to extract prosodic variations but not with the same aptness as a human.

So far our online system only extracts acoustic prosodic features. It comprises speech recognition, prosodic feature extraction, prosodic functionals calculation, word prominence labeling and visual feedback to the user. The speech recognition module decodes what the user has said and performs a word level temporal alignment which is required for the calculation of the prosodic functionals. We decided to use the HARK system developed at Honda Research Institute Japan together with Kyoto University to perform speech recognition [30]. The HARK system enables multi-channel speech enhancement and features the communication with the Julius speech recognition system via TCP/IP sockets [25].

We extended Julius with the possibility to communicate the recognition results and the temporal alignments also via TCP/IP to our RTBOS middelware which allows the component-based development of real-time systems [10]. We perform all remaining steps in our RTBOS framework which in particular allows a flexible distribution of processing modules to threads. For the extraction of the fundamental frequency we use the online implementation of our pitch tracking algorithm detailed in [20]. The extraction of the remaining acoustic features and the calculation of the functionals is straight forward. We have not yet integrated the contour modeling in the online system. For the word prominence labeling we also use in the online system the LibSVM [11].

7 Conclusion

In this paper we demonstrated on one hand how modeling the prosodic contours via FPCA can improve the detection of prominent words. On the other hand we also showed that for some speakers the visual channel can be efficiently used to detect prominent words. In particular we obtained from the head movements alone accuracies clearly above chance level for all speakers. Next we will extend the level of context available to the system by integrating the contour modeling with a decoding of the word sequence [34]. Furthermore, we will investigate how users adapt to a system capable of processing word prominence.

Acknowledgments. I want to thank Petra Wagner, Britta Wrede and Heiko Wersing for fruitful discussions. Furthermore, I am very grateful to Rujiao Yan and Samuel Kevin Ngouoko for helping in setting up the visual processing and the forced alignment, respectively as well to Venkatesh Kulkarni for developing the Voicing Detection. Many thanks to Mark Dunn for support with the cameras and the recording system as well to Mathias Franzius for support with tuning the SVMs and Andrea Schnall, Paschalis Mikias and Merikan Koyun for help in the data preparation. Special thanks go to my subjects for their patience and effort.

References

1. Replaygain 1.0 specification. http://wiki.hydrogenaudio.org/
2. Al Moubayed, S., Beskow, J.: Effects of visual prominence cues on speech intelligibility. In: Proceedings of International Conference on Auditory Visual Speech Process. (AVSP), vol. 9, p. 16. ISCA (2009)
3. Arias, J.P., Busso, C., Yoma, N.B.: Energy and f0 contour modeling with functional data analysis for emotional speech detection. In: Proceedings of INTERSPEECH, Lyon, FR (2013)
4. Arias, J.P., Busso, C., Yoma, N.B.: Shape-based modeling of the fundamental frequency contour for emotion detection in speech. Comput. Speech Lang. **28**(1), 278–294 (2014)
5. Beskow, J., Granström, B., House, D.: Visual correlates to prominence in several expressive modes. In: Proceedings of INTERSPEECH, pp. 1272–1275. ISCA (2006)
6. Black, A., Taylor, P., Caley, R.: The festival speech synthesis system. Technical report (1998)

7. Bradski, G.: The openCV library. Dr. Dobb's J. Softw. Tools **25**, 122–125 (2000)
8. Buendia, A., Devillers, L.: From informative cooperative dialogues to long-term social relation with a robot. In: Mariani, J., Devillers, L., Garnier-Rizet, M., Rosset, S. (eds.) Natural Interaction with Robots, Knowbots and Smartphones - Putting Spoken Dialog Systems into Practice, pp. 135–151. Springer, Heidelberg (2014)
9. Campbell, N.: On the use of nonverbal speech sounds in human communication. In: Esposito, A., Faundez-Zanuy, M., Keller, E., Marinaro, M. (eds.) COST Action 2102. LNCS (LNAI), vol. 4775, pp. 117–128. Springer, Heidelberg (2007)
10. Ceravola, A., Stein, M., Goerick, C.: Researching and developing a real-time infrastructure for intelligent systems - evolution of an integrated approach. Robot. Auton. Syst. **56**(1), 14–28 (2008)
11. Chang, C.C., Lin, C.J.: LIBSVM: a library for support vector machines. ACM Trans. Intell. Syst. Technol. **2**, 27:1–27:27 (2011). http://www.csie.ntu.edu.tw/ cjlin/libsvm
12. Cooke, M., Barker, J., Cunningham, S., Shao, X.: An audio-visual corpus for speech perception and automatic speech recognition. J. Acoust. Soc. Am. **120**, 2421–2424 (2006)
13. Cvejic, E., Kim, J., Davis, C., Gibert, G.: Prosody for the eyes: quantifying visual prosody using guided principal component analysis. In: Proceedings of INTER-SPEECH. ISCA (2010)
14. Dohen, M., Lœvenbruck, H., Harold, H., et al.: Visual correlates of prosodic contrastive focus in french: description and inter-speaker variability. In: Speech Prosody, Dresden, Germany (2006)
15. Eyben, F., Wöllmer, M., Schuller, B.: Opensmile: the munich versatile and fast open-source audio feature extractor. In: Proceedings of International Conference on Multimedia, pp. 1459–1462. ACM (2010)
16. Graf, H., Cosatto, E., Strom, V., Huang, F.: Visual prosody: facial movements accompanying speech. In: International Conference on Automatic Face and Gesture Recognition, pp. 396–401. IEEE (2002)
17. Heckmann, M.: Audio-visual evaluation and detection of word prominence in a human-machine interaction scenario. In: Proceedings of INTERSPEECH. ISCA, Portland (2012)
18. Heckmann, M.: Inter-speaker variability in audio-visual classification of word prominence. In: Proceedings of INTERSPEECH, Lyon, France (2013)
19. Heckmann, M., Domont, X., Joublin, F., Goerick, C.: A closer look on hierarchical spectro-temporal features (HIST). In: Proceedings of INTERSPEECH, Brisbane, Australia (2008)
20. Heckmann, M., Gläser, C., Vaz, M., Rodemann, T., Joublin, F., Goerick, C.: Listen to the parrot: demonstrating the quality of online pitch and formant extraction via feature-based resynthesis. In: Proceedings IEEE/RSJ International Conference on Intelligent Robots and Systems (IROS), Nice (2008)
21. Heckmann, M., Joublin, F., Goerick, C.: Combining rate and place information for robust pitch extraction. In: Proceedings of INTERSPEECH, pp. 2765–2768, Antwerp (2007)
22. Heldner, M.: On the reliability of overall intensity and spectral emphasis as acoustic correlates of focal accents in swedish. J. Phonetics **31**(1), 39–62 (2003)
23. Jeon, J., Wang, W., Liu, Y.: N-best rescoring based on pitch-accent patterns. In: Proceedings of 49th Annual Meeting of the Association for Computational Linguistics: Human Language Technologies, vol. 1, pp. 732–741. Association for Computational Linguistics (2011)

24. Kristjansson, T., Deligne, S., Olsen, P.: Voicing features for robust speech detection. In: Proceedings of INTERSPEECH, vol. 2, p. 3 (2005)
25. Lee, A., Kawahara, T.: Recent development of open-source speech recognition engine julius. In: Proceedings of Asia-Pacific Signal and Information Processing Association Annual Summit and Conference, pp. 131–137 (2009)
26. Levow, G.: Identifying local corrections in human-computer dialogue. In: Eighth International Conference on Spoken Language Processing (ICSLP) (2004)
27. Litman, D., Hirschberg, J., Swerts, M.: Characterizing and predicting corrections in spoken dialogue systems. Comput. Linguist. **32**(3), 417–438 (2006)
28. Michele, G., Torreira, F., Boves, L.: Using FDA for investigating multidimensional dynamic phonetic contrasts. Preprint submitted to Journal of Phonetics (2013)
29. Munhall, K., Jones, J., Callan, D., Kuratate, T., Vatikiotis-Bateson, E.: Visual prosody and speech intelligibility. Psychol. Sci. **15**(2), 133 (2004)
30. Nakadai, K., Okuno, H., Nakajima, H., Hasegawa, Y., Tsujino, H.: An open source software system for robot audition hark and its evaluation. In: Proceedings of IEEE-RAS International Conference on Humanoid Robots (2008)
31. Ramsay, J.: Functions for functional data analysis in R, SPLUS and Matlab. http://www.psych.mcgill.ca/misc/fda/
32. Ramsay, J., Silverman, B.: Functional Data Analysis. Springer, New York (2005)
33. Rosenberg, A.: Automatic detection and classification of prosodic events. Ph.D. thesis, Columbia University (2009)
34. Schnall, A., Heckmann, M.: Integrating sequence information in the audio-visual detection of word prominence in a human-machine interaction scenario. In: Proceedings of INTERSPEECH, Singapore (2014)
35. Schroder, M., Bevacqua, E., Cowie, R., Eyben, F., Gunes, H., Heylen, D., Ter Maat, M., McKeown, G., Pammi, S., Pantic, M., Pelachaud, C., Schuller, B., de Sevin, E., Valstar, M., Wöllmer, M.: Building autonomous sensitive artificial listeners. IEEE Trans. Affect. Comput. **3**(2), 165–183 (2012)
36. Schuller, B., Steidl, S., Batliner, A., Burkhardt, F., Devillers, L., Müller, C., Narayanan, S.: Paralinguistics in speech and languag-state-of-the-art and the challenge. Comput. Speech Lang. **27**(1), 4–39 (2013)
37. Shriberg, E.: Spontaneous speech: How people really talk and why engineers should care. In: Proceedings of EUROSPEECH. ISCA (2005)
38. Shriberg, E., Ferrer, L., Kajarekar, S., Venkataraman, A., Stolcke, A.: Modeling prosodic feature sequences for speaker recognition. Speech Commun. **46**(3), 455–472 (2005)
39. Shriberg, E., Stolcke, A., Hakkani-Tür, D.Z., Heck, L.P.: Learning when to listen: detecting system-addressed speech in human-human-computer dialog. In: Proceedings of INTERSPEECH (2012)
40. Swerts, M., Krahmer, E.: Facial expression and prosodic prominence: effects of modality and facial area. J. Phonetics **36**(2), 219–238 (2008)
41. Swerts, M., Litman, D., Hirschberg, J.: Corrections in spoken dialogue systems. In: Sixth International Conference on Spoken Language Processing (ICSLP). ISCA, Bejing (2000)
42. Wang, D., Narayanan, S.: An acoustic measure for word prominence in spontaneous speech. IEEE Trans. Audio Speech and Lang. Proc. **15**(2), 690–701 (2007)
43. Young, S., Odell, J., Ollason, D., Valtchev, V., Woodland, P.: The HTK Book. Cambridge University, Cambridge (1995)

Improving Robustness Against Environmental Sounds for Directing Attention of Social Robots

Nicolai Bæk Thomsen[✉], Zheng-Hua Tan, Børge Lindberg,
and Søren Holdt Jensen

Department of Electronic Systems, Aalborg University,
Fredrik Bajers Vej 7, 9220 Aalborg, Denmark
nit@es.aau.dk

Abstract. This paper presents a multi-modal system for finding out where to direct the attention of a social robot in a dialog scenario, which is robust against environmental sounds (door slamming, phone ringing etc.) and short speech segments. The method is based on combining voice activity detection (VAD) and sound source localization (SSL) and furthermore apply post-processing to SSL to filter out short sounds. The system is tested against a baseline system in four different real-world experiments, where different sounds are used as interfering sounds. The results are promising and show a clear improvement.

1 Introduction

In the past decade much research has been conducted in the field of human-robot interaction (HRI) [1–3] and especially social robots [4], which are to operate and communicate with persons in different and changing environments, have gained much attention. Many different scenarios arise in this context, however in this work we consider the case where a robot takes part in a dialog with multiple speakers. The key task for a social robot is then to figure out when someone is speaking, where the person is located and whether or not to direct its attention toward the person by turning. In uncontrolled environments like living rooms, offices etc. many different spurious non-speech sounds can occur (door slamming, phone ringing, keyboard sounds etc.), making it important for the robot to distinguish between sounds to ignore and sounds coming from persons demanding the attention of the robot. Unlike humans, robots are often not able to quickly classify an acoustic source as human or non-human using vision due to limited field-of-view and limited turning speed. If this ability is missing the behaviour of the robot may seem unnatural from a perceptional point of view, which is undesirable.

In [1], an anchoring system is proposed, which utilizes microphone array, pan-tilt camera and a laser range finder to locate persons. The system is able to direct attention to a speaker and maintain it, however non-speech interfering

This work is supported by the Danish Council for Independent Research - Technology and Production Sciences under grant number: 1335-00162.

R. Böck et al. (Eds.): MA3HMI 2014 Workshop, LNAI 8757, pp. 25–34, 2015.
DOI: 10.1007/978-3-319-15557-9_3

sounds are not considered and the system is only evaluated for persons talking for approximately 10 s. The work in [5] introduces a term called *audio proto objects*, where sounds are segmented based on energy and grouped by various features to filter out non-speech sounds. Good results are reported for localization, however no results are reported for an actual real-world dialog including interfering non-speech sounds.

In this work we focus on a the sound source localization (SSL) part of the system and use standard method for face detection. We specifically propose a system where a voice activity detector (VAD) and SSL are used to award points to angular intervals spanning $[-90°, 90°]$. These points are accumulated over time, enabling the robot only to react to persistent speech sources.

The outline of the paper is as follows: the baseline system will be described in Sect. 2 followed by a description of the proposed system in Sect. 3. Section 4 states results for both a test of the localization system and test of the complete system in different real-world scenarios. Section 5 concludes on the work and discuss how to proceed.

2   Baseline System

We developed a baseline system which is shown in Fig. 1. It is inherently sequential, where first SSL is used to determine the direction of an acoustic source (if any), and then after having turned face detection is used to verify the source and then possibly adjust further. Face detection is done according to [6] and is implemented using OpenCV.

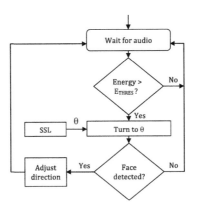

Fig. 1. Flowchart of baseline system.

2.1   Sound Source Localization

For sound source localization (SSL) we use the steered response power method with phase transformation (SRP-PHAT) [7]. It is a generalization of the well-known generalized cross-correlation method with phase transform (GCC-PHAT) [8], when more than one microphone pair is utilized. Furthermore it takes advantage of the whole cross-spectrum and not only the peak value. The basic idea is to form a grid of points (most commonly in spherical coordinates) relative to some point, which is typically the center of the microphone array, and then steer the microphone array toward each point in the grid using delay-sum beamforming and at last find the output power. After all points have been processed, the three-dimensional (azimuth, elevation and distance) power map can now be searched for the maximum value, indicating an acoustic source at that point. It is computationally heavy to consider all points assuming a fine grid of points, however in this work we are only interested in the direction, and not elevation, hence we can disregard this. Assuming that the source is located in the far-field, i.e. the microphone spacing is much smaller than the distance to the source, we can use only one value for distance.

3   Proposed System

Figure 2 shows the structure of the proposed system. It has the same overall sequential structure as the baseline where audio is first used to roughly estimate the direction of the person, and afterwards vision is used to verify the existence of a speaker and possibly adjust the direction further. The two differences between the baseline system and the proposed system are; first, the use of a better VAD to increase robustness against environmental sounds, and second, post-processing of SSL to increase robustness against short speech segments and short sounds, which are misclassified by the VAD.

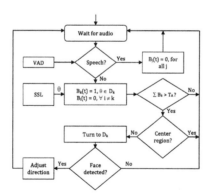

Fig. 2. Flowchart of proposed system. The post-processing using $B_i(t)$ is explained in Sect. 3.2.

3.1   Voice Activity Detection

In this work a variant of the voice activity detector (VAD) described in [9, 10] is utilized. Results show a good trade-off between accuracy and low complexity, which is of high importance, because the robot has limited resources and heavy processing tasks such as image processing and speech recognition (not included in this work) should run simultaneously. The algorithm is based on a posteriori SNR weighted energy difference and involves the following step, which are performed on every audio frame.

1. Compute the a posteriori SNR weighted energy difference given by

$$D(t) = \sqrt{|E(t) - E(t-1)| \cdot \text{SNR}_{\text{post}}(t)} \ . \tag{1}$$

   where $E(t)$ is the logarithmic energy of frame t and $\text{SNR}_{\text{post}}(t)$ is the a posteriori SNR of frame t.
2. Compute the threshold for selecting the frame given by

$$T = \overline{D(t)} \cdot f(\text{SNR}_{\text{post}}(t)) \cdot 0.1 \ . \tag{2}$$

   where $\overline{D(t)}$ is an average of $D(t), D(t-1), ..., D(t-T)$, and $f(\text{SNR}_{\text{post}}(t))$ is piece-wise constant function, such that the threshold is higher for low SNR and lower for high SNR. If $D(t) > T$, then $S(t) = 1$ otherwise $S(t) = 0$.
3. Perform a prior moving average on $S(t)$ and compare to threshold, T_{VAD}. If above threshold, the frame is classified as speech and otherwise as non-speech.

It should be noted that the VAD is only performed on one of the four channels from the microphone array.

3.2   Post-processing of SSL

The range of output angles, $[-90°, 90°]$, from SSL is divided into non-overlapping regions, e.g. the first region could be $D_1 = [-90°, -85°[$. This is motivated by the fact that even during short speech segments ($\sim$1 s) the speaker is not standing completely still and likewise the head is also not completely fixed, thus SSL estimates which are very close should not be assigned to different sources, but are most likely to be caused by the same source. In this work we have split the range of angles into regions of $5°$ except for the center region which is defined as $[-5°, 5°[$, thus the total number of regions is 35. For each of the aforementioned regions we assign a vector $\boldsymbol{B}_i(t) = [B_i(t-T+1) \ B_i(t-T+2) \ ... \ B_i(t)]$, where t denotes the tth audio frame and T denotes the length of the vector in terms of audio frames. Whenever an audio frame is classified as speech by the VAD, SSL is used to estimate the angle of the supposed speaker relative to the robot. The current element of the vector corresponding to the region, in which the estimated angle belongs, is then set to 1 for the current frame, t, and all current elements of vectors for the other regions are set to 0. If the frame is classified as non-speech, then the current element of all vectors are set to 0. Attention is then given to region i if the sum of the corresponding vector is above some threshold, i.e. $\sum_{m=T-1}^{0} B_i(t-m) > T_A$. If a vector exceeds the threshold thus making the robot turn, the vectors for all regions are set to zero. The motivation for this system is that it enables control over the duration of the sentences which should trigger the robot to turn toward a speaker.

4 Evaluation of the Systems

Two seperate test were performed. One test with the purpose of testing only the localization capabilities of both baseline and proposed system and that the robot was able to turn toward the sound source and adjust using vision, and a second test where the system was tested in four different types of scenarios with three speakers and interfering sounds.

4.1 Localization Performance

We test only the proposed system here, since for one speaker and no noise they are the same. The localization system was tested for five different angles by having a person speaking continuously at the angle at a distance of approximately 1.5 m until the robot had turned toward the person. Here the angle between robot and person is defined as in Fig. 3, where positive angles are clockwise. The results are stated in Table 1. It is seen that the system is clearly able to turn toward the person with acceptable accuracy. It should be noted that this test is associated with some uncertainties, since it is very difficult to place the speaker at the exact angle, and it is difficult to measure the angle with high accuracy.

Table 1. Performance of localization system. Mean and standard deviation of angle between person and robot after localization and rotation. 10 repetitions were used for each angle.

	15°	30°	45°	60°	75°
μ	14.2	29.1	45.9	59.1	73.4
σ	0.9	1.3	1.3	0.9	2.7

4.2 Attention System Performance

The baseline and proposed system were tested through four different experiments, resulting in a total of eight trials. The four experiments are described below

1. The speakers take turn talking for approximately 10 s.
2. The speakers take turn talking for approximately 10 s and in between speakers interfering sounds are played (see Table 2).
3. The speakers take turn talking for either approximately 10 s or 1 s.
4. The speakers take turn talking for either approximately 10 s or 1 s and in between speakers interfering sounds are played (see Table 2).

In all four experiments a total of 20 time slots are used, where a slot can either be a speaker talking (10 s or 1 s) or an interfering sound, thus the slots are of varying length. We emphasize that there is no overlapping sounds. Information about the interfering sounds is listed in Table 2. Each noise source is responsible for two different sounds, where sound 1 is always played as the first of the two.

Table 2. Description of the six interfering sounds used in the experiments. Same ringtone used for both sound 1 and sound 2 from N3.

Source	Sound 1			Sound 2		
	Description	Duration	SPL (dB)	Description	Duration	SPL (dB)
N1	Coughing	≈0.7 s	≈77 dB	Door slamming	≈0.4 s	≈90 dB
N2	Scrambling chair	≈1.1 s	≈80 dB	Scrambling chair	≈1.1 s	≈89 dB
N3	Phone ringing	≈3.7 s	≈75 dB	Phone ringing	≈3.7 s	≈75 dB

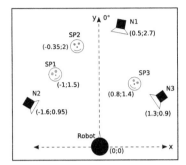

Fig. 3. Setup for attention experiment. XY-coordinates are given in metres.

The test setup and the location of the robot, the noise sources and the speakers are shown in Fig. 3. All experiments were recorded using a seperate microphone and a seperate video camera and information about the direction of the robot was logged on the robot. This data was afterwards used to annotate precisely when different sounds occurred, and the focus of attention of the robot was also annotated using this. The logged data from the robot was not used directly, as the absolute angle did not match reality due to small offsets in the base when turning, however it was used for determining the timeline precisely. We also emphasize that the annotation of a sound begins when the sound begins and is extended until the next sound begins, thus silence is not explicitly stated due to simplicity. Furthermore, the annotation of the robot starts when the robots has settled at a direction, thus turning is not stated explicitly. Figures 4, 5, 6, and 7 show the results for the four experiments for both baseline and proposed system, where "OOC" means out-of-category, "SP1" means speaker 1, "N1" means noise source 1 and so on. "Annotation" (light grey) shows who was active/speaking and "Robot" (black) shows where the attention of the robot was focused.

Table 3 states the number of correct and incorrect transitions along with number of anomalous behaviours. A correct transition is when the robot turns attention to a person speaking for approximately 10 s or ignores a short speech segment (approximately 1 s) or an interfering sound. An example of the first case is seen in Fig. 5(b) at the start, where the robot turns toward SP3. An example of the second is seen in the same figure at slot 1 to 2, where the robot does not shift attention due to an interfering sound from noise source N1. An incorrect

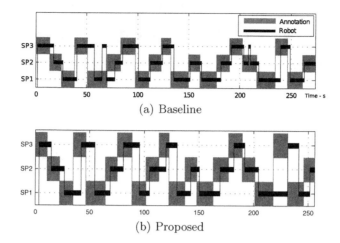

(a) Baseline

(b) Proposed

Fig. 4. Experiment 1. Figure 4(a) shows the baseline and Fig. 4(b) shows the performance of the proposed method. The two anomalous behaviours for the baseline are assumed to be caused by sounds, not related to the experiment, created from the direction of SP3. The much delayed transition in the proposed system in the end is caused by not triggering the VAD properly.

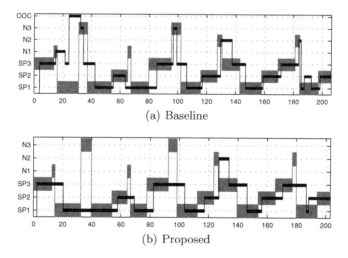

(a) Baseline

(b) Proposed

Fig. 5. Experiment 2. Legends and axis similar to Fig. 4. It is seen that for the baseline the robot turns toward SP3 after N3, which is due to detecting the face of SP3. A similar thing happens for both the baseline and proposed system in the second last time slot. We also note that the VAD used in the proposed method is triggered by the "sound 1" from N2 at ~125 s, which is unexpected, however this could most likely be avoided using pitch information too.

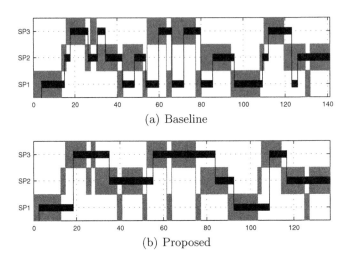

(a) Baseline

(b) Proposed

Fig. 6. Experiment 3. Legends and axis similar to Fig. 4. The anomalous behaviour for the baseline in the third last slot is caused by detecting the face of SP1.

transition is when the robot turns toward a noise source, a person speaking for approximately 1 s or out-of-category. The number of correct and incorrect transitions should add to 20. An anomalous behaviour is when the robot makes an unexpected turn during a slot. An example is seen in Fig. 5(b) in slot 19, where the robot turns toward SP2 while SP3 is speaking. We see in Table 3 that for the first experiment both systems perform equally well, which is too be expected. But as both short sentences and interfering sounds are added to the experiment, the proposed method generally performs better than the baseline. The relatively low number of correct transitions for both the baseline and the proposed method in experiment 4 is caused by being adressed by a speaker from a relative angle greater than $|90|°$, which is a general limitation of the SSL algorithm used in both systems.

Table 3. Number of correct and incorrect transitions and anomalous behaviours for the baseline and the proposed system for each experiment.

Experiment	Baseline			Proposed		
	#Correct	#Incorrect	#Anomalies	#Correct	#Incorrect	#Anomalies
1	20	0	2	19	1	0
2	13	7	3	18	2	1
3	12	8	1	20	0	0
4	8	12	0	14	6	3

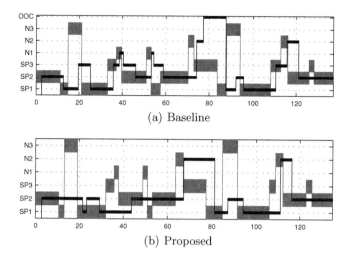

(a) Baseline

(b) Proposed

Fig. 7. Experiment 4. Legends and axis similar to Fig. 4. In the beginning of the baseline, the robot turns toward SP3 instead of N3. This happens because N3 is located at an angle of $\sim +90°$ relative to SP1, and since the SSL has lower resolution for large angles, the sound is perceived as coming from a smaller angle. It is seen that both systems behaves unexpectedly at $t \sim 75\,s$. This is caused by the fact, that SSL only covers $[-90°, 90°]$. Again, the VAD in the proposed system is triggered by the sounds from N2, which is undesirable.

5 Conclusion

In this work we have presented a method for increasing robustness against environmental sounds and short speech segments for sound source localization in the context of a social robot. Different experiments have been conducted and they show an improvement over a baseline system. The method proposed is however based on a constant, T_A, set before deployment of the robot, which is not ideal. Future work should look into how this parameter can be learned during runtime. Furthermore, using a VAD designed for distant speech would improve the system.

Acknowledgements. Authors would like to thank Xiaodong Duan for great help on setting up experiments and implementing face detection.

References

1. Lang, S., Kleinehagenbrock, M., Hohenner, S., Fritsch, J., Fink, G.A., Sagerer, G.: Providing the basis for human-robot-interaction: a multi-modal attention system for a mobile robot. In: Proceedings of the International Conference on Multimodal Interfaces, pp. 28–35. ACM (2003)

2. Song, K.-T., Hu, J.-S., Tsai, C.-Y., Chou, C.-M., Cheng, C.-C., Liu, W.-H., Yang, C.-H.: Speaker attention system for mobile robots using microphone array and face tracking. In: Proceedings 2006 IEEE International Conference on Robotics and Automation, 2006, ICRA 2006, May 2006, pp. 3624–3629 (2006)

3. Stiefelhagen, R., Ekenel, H., Fugen, C., Gieselmann, P., Holzapfel, H., Kraft, F., Nickel, K., Voit, M., Waibel, A.: Enabling multimodal human robot interaction for the karlsruhe humanoid robot. IEEE Trans. Robot. **23**(5), 840–851 (2007)

4. Malfaz, M., Castro-Gonzalez, A., Barber, R., Salichs, M.: A biologically inspired architecture for an autonomous and social robot. IEEE Trans. Auton. Ment. Dev. **3**(3), 232–246 (2011)

5. Rodemann, T., Joublin, F., Goerick, C.: Audio proto objects for improved sound localization. In: IEEE/RSJ International Conference on Intelligent Robots and Systems, 2009, IROS 2009, Oct 2009, pp. 187–192 (2009)

6. Viola, P., Jones, M.: Robust real-time object detection. International Journal of Computer Vision (2001)

7. Dmochowski, J., Benesty, J., Affes, S.: A generalized steered response power method for computationally viable source localization. IEEE Trans. Audio Speech Lang. Process. **15**(8), 2510–2526 (2007)

8. Knapp, C., Carter, G.C.: The generalized correlation method for estimation of time delay. IEEE Trans. Acoust. Speech Signal Process. **24**(4), 320–327 (1976)

9. Tan, Z.-H., Lindberg, B.: Low-complexity variable frame rate analysis for speech recognition and voice activity detection. IEEE J. Sel. Top. Sign. Process. **4**(5), 798–807 (2010)

10. Plchot, O., Matsoukas, S., Matejka, P., Dehak, N., Ma, J., Cumani, S., Glembek, O., Hermansky, H., Mallidi, S., Mesgarani, N., Schwartz, R., Soufifar, M., Tan, Z., Thomas, S., Zhang, B., Zhou, X.: Developing a speaker identification system for the darpa rats project. In: 2013 IEEE International Conference on Acoustics, Speech and Signal Processing (ICASSP), May 2013, pp. 6768–6772 (2013)

On Annotation and Evaluation of Multi-modal Corpora in Affective Human-Computer Interaction

Markus Kächele[(⊠)], Martin Schels, Sascha Meudt, Viktor Kessler,
Michael Glodek, Patrick Thiam, Stephan Tschechne, Günther Palm,
and Friedhelm Schwenker

Institute of Neural Information Processing, Ulm University,
James-Franck-Ring, 89081 Ulm, Germany
markus.kaechele@uni-ulm.de

Abstract. In this paper, we discuss the topic of affective human-computer interaction from a data driven viewpoint. This comprises the collection of respective databases with emotional contents, feasible annotation procedures and software tools that are able to conduct a suitable labeling process. A further issue that is discussed in this paper is the evaluation of the results that are computed using statistical classifiers. Based on this we propose to use fuzzy memberships in order to model affective user state and endorse respective fuzzy performance measures.

Keywords: Affective computing · Annotation · Machine learning · Human computer interaction · Multimodal corpora · Fuzzy memberships

1 Introduction

Research on human-computer interaction (HCI) has undergone a dramatic change from the pure investigations on how the interaction of humans with computers should best take place and instead started to focus on how computers should react to human operators. Therefore new means of communication are investigated such as visual communicational cues of humans, nonverbal communication (not necessarily the content of what is said) and physiological measurements from the body of the user. Research suggests that the affective state of a human is communicated willingly and unwillingly through several channels with many of them allowing direct inference through sensory measurements. It has been shown that different modalities such as audio [9,13,14,22], video [7,21] and also bio-physiology [10,19] can convey different aspects of the affective state. Measurements based on single modalities however are prone to noise, artifacts (e.g. missing sensor input) and other difficulties (e.g. specific minimum lengths of time windows). Therefore the combination of different channels in a sequence of interaction has been attracting increasing attention and experiments have shown to be promising [5,16–18,36].

© Springer International Publishing Switzerland 2015
R. Böck et al. (Eds.): MA3HMI 2014 Workshop, LNAI 8757, pp. 35–44, 2015.
DOI: 10.1007/978-3-319-15557-9_4

However, in order to work properly, the respective statistical machine learning approaches have to be trained using examples of the emotions and affective states that are targeted. For this task, datasets are needed that already contain proper instances of the respective affective states of feasible qualities and quantities to make it possible to extract meaningful statistics. The affective states should occur in sequences of sufficient length with enough repetitions to capture potential time dependencies [4] and in equally balanced quantities [8] to prevent training of biased classifiers. The generation of datasets including accurate knowledge about the respective affective states and how they appear is the key to data driven affective computing. However, this task is by no means trivial and the induction of affective states, the recording and most importantly the annotation of the data and even the evaluation of the performance of the results are very challenging.

Therefore, this work tries to establish a guideline that sheds light on the problems and difficulties that come with the definition of proper affective states for a given task, the conception of multi-modal affective corpora, and most importantly the reliable annotation of the recorded data to fit in the problem formulation. The discussed problems include time dependencies, proper handling of multiple raters, and appropriate measures of performance of classification systems given arbitrary label signals.

The remainder of this work is organized as follows. In the next section, annotation techniques are presented and an analysis of their advantages and use-cases are presented. In Sect. 2, an overview over well-known multi-modal corpora is given together with a characterization of their ground truth label information. Subsequently, the necessary tools available for data annotation are discussed in Sect. 4. In Sect. 5, commonly used performance measures are reviewed before the last Section concludes the paper with a discussion and an outlook on open issues.

2   Labeling Techniques

A further non-trivial issue for the assembly of affective corpora is the annotation of the recorded materials with labels that reflect a user's state adequately. There are mainly three different approaches that are followed to assign labels in this application, that try to circumvent the fact that the true state is commonly unknown and also not exactly assessable.

The most straightforward approach to determine the affective state is to query it from the respective subject. For this purpose different questionnaires and pictographic techniques have been developed to infer emotional states. It is however not really possible to reflect short or medium term changes of affective states using this technique as it is desirable for human-computer interaction scenarios.

One rather popular method is to design different external stimuli that are presented to the test subject in a carefully pre-defined order to elicit a desired affective state [15,35]. This comprises for example different difficulties of a given task or making the interaction with the technical system more difficult, e.g., by impairing the reactions to commands of the user to the computer. Thus, the

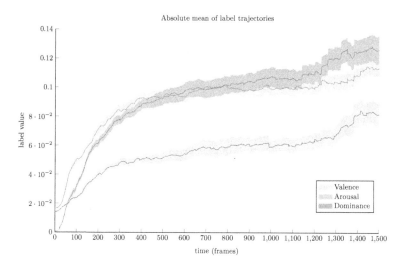

Fig. 1. Average VAD labels of a continuously annotated multi-modal corpus. The trajectories seem to exhibit a transient phase starting at an arbitrary zero level and begin to climb to the actual value range of the respective label. The variances (lighter colored corridors) are very small in the beginning which indicates that almost every rater immediately started to leave the zero level. It should be considered to discard transient phases in the beginning of an annotation process.

different target states can be identified in the temporal order of the interaction that is given by the experimental protocol.

An alternative to that approach is to manually label the material after the recording step is conducted [25,30,33]. As mentioned before, it is very difficult to infer an emotional state of a subject from the outside when the affective display is only subtle. Hence a large number of naive raters is required in order to average out the errors that the individual raters are assumed to commit. Having a large amount of raters can indeed be highly profitable as for example presented in [32]. The authors published the results of an experiment where untrained users from the Internet could sign up and annotate images in a web-based application over an extended period of time. Surprisingly, the users contributed a large set of valuable annotations spanning a large variety of object and scene classes. The authors emphasize the accuracy provided by the group of untrained annotators: An extraction of 3-D coordinates from multiple views gained from user annotations was comparable to the quality produced by laser range scanners. However, procedures like this are very cost intensive and sometimes not possible.

A further issue is that there is not really a convenient procedure for the manual annotation to process. Using a continuous annotation method where a label value is manipulated in real time potentially renders a comparably fast annotation method but might suffer from the individual mindfulness and the reaction times of the respective rater. A further observation in this context is that now not only the temporal order of the conducted experiment is influencing possible labels, but also the constraints of the respective label tool influence the annotation. In Fig. 1 an illustrative example for this problem is shown that depicts initial transient phases that occur in the beginning of the recordings. It can be seen that almost every rater immediately left the baseline and progressed towards non-zero values of the respective label, which might not necessarily reflect the true state of the subject. This problem can be solved by discarding transient phases or by randomly rearranging the sequences of the recording to obtain annotations for the whole recording.

The annotation of categorical labels is even more complex and requires commonly a large amount of navigating in the assigned material [12,23].

3 Data Collections Comprising Affective HCI

Notable multi-modal data collections that have been constructed in the application of human-computer interaction are outlined in the following.

The *last minute* corpus is designed to study affective human-computer dialogs [15], having audio-visual material. A test subject is instructed to gather a suitcase for a voyage via airplane using a voice controlled computer interface. Different user states are elicited using malfunctions in the dialog system and unexpected events in the recording. Different time slots in the interaction sequences constitute labels that are passed to automatic classification.

The *EmoRec II* corpus is also collected to study emotions in human-computer interaction [34], comprising audio, video and physiological data material [20]. In this data collection test subjects were instructed to play multiple games of Concentration using a voice controlled interface which is operated in a Wizard-of-Oz protocol. Different emotions in the Valence-Arousal-Dominance (VAD) space were induced using different difficulties of the game and negative or positive feedback from the system. Sequences of similar stimuli were considered as blocks of the same label in the VAD space [19].

The *AVEC 2011 and 2012* [27] data collections comprise audio-visual sequences of more or less free interaction with an artificial avatar, which is designed to elicit different affective states. The individual recordings were annotated by multiple human labelers in four different affective dimensions: Arousal, Expectancy, Power and Valence. The AVEC 2011 corpus comprises binarized label traces whereas for the 2012 edition of the competition continuous labels are provided.

The *AVEC 2013 and 2014* [33] corpora move in a sense away from the human-computer interaction scenario to a clinical environment with test subjects suffering from different levels of depression. The patients, that were recorded using camera and microphones, were instructed to conduct different, in parts therapeutic, tasks such as talking about their childhood but also reading pre-defined texts. The data is annotated using two different paradigms: first a medical questionnaire procedure is conducted to infer the depressive state and the data is also manually annotated by one to five human annotators in different continuous affective categories, namely Arousal and Valence for the 2013 edition and Valence, Arousal and Dominance for the 2014 edition.

The *PIT corpus* [30] conducts a more explorative approach to the subject of human-computer interaction by enabling a computer assisted multi party dialog, where two users are choosing a restaurant they can agree on. The corpus was used to develop a set of labels that are useful for the human-computer interaction such as high level categories (e.g., interest in the interaction with the machine) and also low level properties (e.g., is the user looking at the computer screen). Audio and video from multiple camera angles are provided with the data collection.

A further multi-modal interaction corpus is described in [28] with the goal of investigating multi-modal interaction history of subjects within a HCI scenario. The interaction consisted of solving puzzles of varying difficulties using predefined interaction modalities such as speech, touch and mouse input. The audio-visual recordings show spontaneous reactions in response to the given feedback during the puzzle solving. Interesting events such as smiles, frowns, head shaking or shouting were manually labeled using the ATLAS tool into the 2 categories *neutral* and *event*. The expressiveness of the different subjects was highly distributed over the whole spectrum and an incentive in the form of a variable amount of money dependent on the performance of the subject was used to amplify the reactions.

4 Tools for Manual Annotation

The tool, which is used to gather the ground truth of a dataset, the annotation process itself and the way the data is presented influences the result of the annotation. For example human annotators tend to accept suggestions made by the system even if they are not sure in their decision. In the following we will discuss several state-of-the-art annotation tools in the affective computing community.

Feeltrace is a freely available fully continuous labeling tool for two emotional dimensions at a time [2]. It supports the annotation of audio and video files and was used for the annotation, e.g. of the continuous AVEC challenges. The annotation is done in real time with an retail joystick whose two axes correspond to the two emotional axes. Hence, there strong correlations between the two annotations which is might not be supported by the underlying dataset.Another drawback is given by the starting point of the annotated curve, which might be arbitrarily set at the starting point of a video.

Anvil, an annotation-tool, was originally developed in 2000 and supports audio and video material [11]. It is generally designed for the crisp annotation of HCI sequences including anthropology, psychotherapy, embodied agents, oceanography corpora, and also supports 3D motion capturing.Hierarchical label definitions and annotations are supported by the definition of respective labels. Some minor analysis tools are included such as histograms of labels, automatic computation of agreement between raters.

Ikannotate is a freely available annotation tool for audio data [1]. It provides an annotation interface for BE and crisp GEW labels. In addition a Self Assessment Manikins solution (SAM) in the VAD space is provided. Additionally, the given audio material can be transcribed according to GAT1/2, which is very unique in compared to other tools.

An alternative in the field of audio annotation is given by EmoWheel [26]. As label space the GEW is used, it is further possible to annotate the data in a continuous space, by assigning a beta distribution. This gives a hint of the course of an emotional expression. One disadvantage is in fact the assumed distribution of the emotional intensity, restricting it to have a global maximum.

ATLAS is specialized in the annotation of datasets containing multiple data streams like audio and video streams, bio-physiological data or more general any kind of $(t \times \mathbb{R}^d)$ data as for example features or classification results [12]. It is freely available and developed at the University of Ulm. All imported data can be displayed and investigated at the same time, which gives researchers an overview over the whole dataset. Adaptive visibility can be used to focus on a specialized topic. The user interface and the label scheme are designed generically, which renders a flexible and powerful technology to display the data material. For the annotation of very large amounts of data a distributed annotation process is in development. To assist the annotator in his work an active learning module is included. In this module feature tracks (or more general, data tracks) can be combined with label tracks in order to obtain label suggestions. These suggestions can either be accepted or rejected by the annotators in an iterative process, to dramatically accelerate the annotation process by simultaneously improving the quality.

5 Performance Measures

The training of feasible classifiers for the recognition of affect in HCI scenarios heavily depends on the characteristics of the ground truth labels and on adequate performance measures to assess the quality of the respective classifiers.

In discrete multi-class problems, the performance measure of choice is usually the accuracy defined as the fraction of correctly classified samples and all available samples. This measure is very intuitive and easily computed, but in this respective application the definition of crisp labels for affective categories seems to neglect the inherent complexity of the matter: It is rather obvious that emotional states occur in varying characteristics and also in different levels of certainty.

This makes it appealing to use continuous label schemata in order to model affective states gradually. Corresponding measures for the assessment of the congruence of two trajectories to assess the quality of an estimation have been proposed for standard regression tasks in the literature. Natural choices include measuring the per time step difference of the trajectories like the absolute mean (MAE) or the root mean squared error (RMSE). Another measure is Pearson's correlation coefficient, that quantifies the linear interconnection of measurements. A high performance value of a prediction is thus defined for potentially rather different curves by these measures. Precisely, using the MAE, a high correspondence for trajectories that overlap to a great extent is favored, leading

to small individual differences at each time step. If the RMSE is used a similar behavior is observed but outliers and huge deviations are penalized much
larger. The correlation coefficient on the other hand focuses on the course of the
trajectory – exact matching of the individual values is not necessary for a high
performance. In Fig. 2, this problem is illustrated by the means of the labels
for the AVEC 2014 corpus: The predicted value of the label arousal (blue line)
matches in most of the cases exactly the true label (red line) as seen in Fig. 2(a),
which is not the case in Fig. 2(b) for the same true label curve. However, a by
far higher correlation coefficient is obtained in the second case. This means that
using this kind of continuous annotation makes a more subtle labeling possible
but the respective performance measures are unfortunately rather unintuitive
and ambiguous.

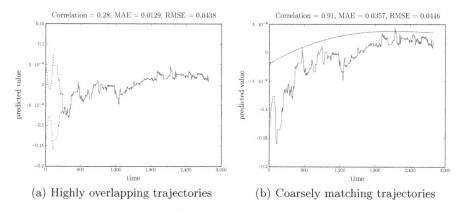

(a) Highly overlapping trajectories   (b) Coarsely matching trajectories

Fig. 2. The left sub-figure illustrates a situation in which the output of a classifier
(blue) exactly matches a given label trajectory except for a transient condition in the
beginning. Computing the correlation between the two curves yields a value of 0.28
despite the curves being almost identical. The right sub-figure illustrates a contrary
example in which the same label is very coarsely estimated by a classifier (again blue).
The computed correlation between the curves results in a rather high value of 0.91
although the ground truth curve is touched only occasionally. The coarsely matching
trajectory however is enough to yield a high correlation with the label. MAE and RMSE
values are also given. Adapted from [6] (Color figure online).

Hence a labeling paradigm and together with a feasible and intuitive performance measure is still missing that particularly reflects the gradual nature
of the human affect over a time period. We propose to use fuzzy memberships
for the different affective classes to measure and quantify the emotional state of
a subject. This framework provides a proper theoretical basis to express uncer-
tainty about a state and also provides powerful statistical classification tools to
process these kinds of information [29, 31]. Further, there is a significant research
effort for the annotation of fuzzy membership values for example using continuous controllers. There are also performance measures that account to fuzzy

memberships, e.g., the fuzzy S_1 measure described in [3], which is defined as $S_1(l^a, l^b) = \frac{\sum_{i=1}^{L} \min(l_i^a, k_i^b)}{\sum_{i=1}^{L} \max(l_i^a, k_i^b)}$. This framework has been already successfully applied to voice quality classification in [24].

6   Summary and Conclusion

In this work the challenges and difficulties of the creation and annotation of multi-modal corpora in the domain of human computer interaction and affective computing were discussed. Challenges comprise the conception of emotional states useful for a given task and the design of adequate multi-modal corpora that contain those states in a sufficient quality and quantity. The different ways the annotation process can be carried out were reviewed and the pitfalls that come with them were highlighted and possible workarounds were given.

To conclude it can be said that there is still a need for affective annotation schemes and respective performance measures that provide both, the capability to allow subtle annotations (which reflects the complexity of the application) and also a certain level of intuition. The usage of fuzzy memberships together with according performance measures provide that to a certain degree.

Acknowledgements. This paper is based on work done within the Transregional Collaborative Research Centre SFB/TRR 62 *Companion-Technology for Cognitive Technical Systems* funded by the German Research Foundation (DFG). The work of Markus Kächele is supported by a scholarship of the Landesgraduiertenförderung Baden-Württemberg at Ulm University.

References

1. Böck, R., Siegert, I., Haase, M., Lange, J., Wendemuth, A.: ikannotate – a tool for labelling, transcription, and annotation of emotionally coloured speech. In: D'Mello, S., Graesser, A., Schuller, B., Martin, J.-C. (eds.) ACII 2011, Part I. LNCS, vol. 6974, pp. 25–34. Springer, Heidelberg (2011)
2. Cowie, R., Douglas-Cowie, E., Savvidou, S., McMahon, E., Sawey, M., Schröder, M.: 'FEELTRACE': an instrument for recording perceived emotion in real time. In: Proceedings of the ISCA Workshop on Speech and Emotion, pp. 19–24 (2000)
3. Dubois, D., Prade, H.: Fuzzy Sets and Systems: Theory and Applications. Academic Press, New York (1980)
4. Glodek, M., Schels, M., Schwenker, F., Palm, G.: Combination of sequential class distributions from multiple channels using markov fusion networks. J. Multimodal User Interfaces **8**, 257–272 (2014)
5. Kächele, M., Glodek, M., Zharkov, D., Meudt, S., Schwenker, F.: Fusion of audio-visual features using hierarchical classifier systems for the recognition of affective states and the state of depression. In: Proceedings of ICPRAM, pp. 671–678 (2014)
6. Kächele, M., Schels, M., Schwenker, F.: Inferring depression and affect from application dependent meta knowledge. In: Proceedings of MM. ACM (2014). http://dx.doi.org/10.1145/2661806.2661813

7. Kächele, M., Schwenker, F.: Cascaded fusion of dynamic, spatial, and textural feature sets for person-independent facial emotion recognition. In: Proceedings of ICPR (2014, to appear)

8. Kächele, M., Thiam, P., Palm, G., Schwenker, F.: Majority-class aware support vector domain oversampling for imbalanced classification problems. In: El Gayar, N., Schwenker, F., Suen, C. (eds.) ANNPR 2014. LNCS, vol. 8774, pp. 83–92. Springer, Heidelberg (2014)

9. Kächele, M., Zharkov, D., Meudt, S., Schwenker, F.: Prosodic, spectral and voice quality feature selection using a long-term stopping criterion for audio-based emotion recognition. In: Proceedings of ICPR (2014, to appear)

10. Kim, J., André, E.: Emotion recognition based on physiological changes in music listening. IEEE Trans. Pattern Anal. Machine Intell. **30**(12), 2067–2083 (2008)

11. Kipp, M.: Anvil - a generic annotation tool for multimodal dialogue. In: Proceedings of 7th European Conference on Speech Communication and Technology (Eurospeech), pp. 1367–1370 (2001)

12. Meudt, S., Bigalke, L., Schwenker, F.: ATLAS - an annotation tool for HCI data utilizing machine learning methods. In: Proceedings of the 1st International Conference on Affective and Pleasurable Design, pp. 5347–5352 (2012)

13. Meudt, S., Zharkov, D., Kächele, M., Schwenker, F.: Multi classifier systems and forward backward feature selection algorithms to classify emotional coloured speech. In: Proceedings of ICMI, pp. 551–556 (2013)

14. Rabiner, L., Juang, B.H.: Fundamentals of Speech Recognition. Prentice Hall, Eaglewood Cliffs (1993)

15. Rösner, D., Frommer, J., Friesen, R., Haase, M., Lange, J., Otto, M.: LAST MINUTE: a multimodal corpus of speech-based user-companion interactions. In: Proceedings of LREC, pp. 2559–2566 (2012)

16. Schels, M., Glodek, M., Meudt, S., Scherer, S., Schmidt, M., Layher, G., Tschechne, S., Brosch, T., Hrabal, D., Walter, S., Traue, H., Palm, G., Neumann, H., Schwenker, F.: Multi-modal classifier-fusion for the recognition of emotions. In: Rojc, M., Campbell, N. (eds.) Coverbal Synchrony in Human-Machine Interaction, pp. 73–98. CRC Press, Boca Raton (2013)

17. Schels, M., Glodek, M., Meudt, S., Schmidt, M., Hrabal, D., Böck, R., Walter, S., Schwenker, F.: Multi-modal classifier-fusion for the classification of emotional states in WOZ scenarios. In: Proceedings of 1st International Conference on Affective and Pleasurable Design, pp. 5337–5346 (2012)

18. Schels, M., Glodek, M., Palm, G., Schwenker, F.: Revisiting AVEC 2011 – an information fusion architecture. In: Apolloni, B., Bassis, S., Esposito, A., Morabito, F.C. (eds.) Neural Nets and Surroundings. SIST, vol. 19, pp. 385–393. Springer, Heidelberg (2013)

19. Schels, M., Kächele, M., Glodek, M., Hrabal, D., Walter, S., Schwenker, F.: Using unlabeled data to improve classification of emotional states in human computer interaction. J. Multimodal User Interfaces **8**(1), 5–16 (2014)

20. Schels, M., Kächele, M., Hrabal, D., Walter, S., Traue, H.C., Schwenker, F.: Classification of emotional states in a Woz scenario exploiting labeled and unlabeled bio-physiological data. In: Schwenker, F., Trentin, E. (eds.) PSL 2011. LNCS, vol. 7081, pp. 138–147. Springer, Heidelberg (2012)

21. Schels, M., Schwenker, F.: A multiple classifier system approach for facial expressions in image sequences utilizing GMM supervectors. In: Proceedings of ICPR, pp. 4251–4254. IEEE (2010)

22. Scherer, K.R., Johnstone, T., Klasmeyer, G.: Affective science. In: Davidson, R.J., Scherer, K.R., Goldsmith, H.H. (eds.) Handbook of Affective Sciences - Vocal expression of Emotion, pp. 433–456. Oxford University Press, New York (2003)

23. Scherer, S., Glodek, M., Layher, G., Schels, M., Schmidt, M., Brosch, T., Tschechne, S., Schwenker, F., Neumann, H., Palm, G.: A generic framework for the inference of user states in human computer interaction: how patterns of low level communicational cues support complex affective states. JMUI **6**(3–4), 117–141 (2012)

24. Scherer, S., Kane, J., Gobl, C., Schwenker, F.: Investigating fuzzy-input fuzzy-output support vector machines for robust voice quality classification. Comput. Speech Lang. **27**(1), 263–287 (2012)

25. Scherer, S., Schels, M., Palm, G.: How low level observations can help to reveal the user's state in HCI. In: D'Mello, S., Graesser, A., Schuller, B., Martin, J.-C. (eds.) ACII 2011, Part II. LNCS, vol. 6975, pp. 81–90. Springer, Heidelberg (2011)

26. Scherer, S., Siegert, I., Bigalke, L., Meudt, S.: Developing an expressive speech labeling tool incorporating the temporal characteristics of emotion. In: Proceedings of LREC, pp. 1172–1175 (2010)

27. Schuller, B., Valstar, M., Eyben, F., McKeown, G., Cowie, R., Pantic, M.: AVEC 2011–the first international audio/visual emotion challenge. In: D'Mello, S., Graesser, A., Schuller, B., Martin, J.-C. (eds.) ACII 2011, Part II. LNCS, vol. 6975, pp. 415–424. Springer, Heidelberg (2011)

28. Schüssel, F., Honold, F., Schmidt, M., Bubalo, N., Huckauf, A., Weber, M.: Multimodal interaction history and its use in error detection and recovery. In: Proceedings of ICMI. ACM (2014, to appear)

29. Schwenker, F., Frey, M., Glodek, M., Kächele, M., Meudt, S., Schels, M., Schmidt, M.: A new multi-class fuzzy support vector machine algorithm. In: El Gayar, N., Schwenker, F., Suen, C. (eds.) ANNPR 2014. LNCS, vol. 8774, pp. 153–164. Springer, Heidelberg (2014)

30. Strauß, P.M., Hoffmann, H., Minker, W., Neumann, H., Palm, G., Scherer, S., Schwenker, F., Traue, H., Walter, W., Weidenbacher, U.: Wizard-of-oz data collection for perception and interaction in multi-user environments. In: Proceedings of LREC, pp. 2014–2017 (2006)

31. Thiel, C., Scherer, S., Schwenker, F.: Fuzzy-input fuzzy-output one-against-all support vector machines. In: Apolloni, B., Howlett, R.J., Jain, L. (eds.) KES 2007, Part III. LNCS (LNAI), vol. 4694, pp. 156–165. Springer, Heidelberg (2007)

32. Torralba, A., Russell, B., Yuen, J.: Labelme: online image annotation and applications. Proc. IEEE **98**(8), 1467–1484 (2010)

33. Valstar, M., Schuller, B., Smith, K., Almaev, T., Eyben, F., Krajewski, J., Cowie, R., Pantic, M.: AVEC 2014: 3D dimensional affect and depression recognition challenge. In: Proceedings of ACM Multimedia 2014. ACM (2014)

34. Walter, S., Kim, J., Hrabal, D., Crawcour, S., Kessler, H., Traue, H.: Transsituational individual-specific biopsychological classification of emotions. IEEE Trans. Syst. Man Cybern. **43**(4), 988–995 (2013)

35. Walter, S., Scherer, S., Schels, M., Glodek, M., Hrabal, D., Schmidt, M., Böck, R., Limbrecht, K., Traue, H.C., Schwenker, F.: Multimodal emotion classification in naturalistic user behavior. In: Jacko, J.A. (ed.) Human-Computer Interaction, Part III, HCII 2011. LNCS, vol. 6763, pp. 603–611. Springer, Heidelberg (2011)

36. Wöllmer, M., Kaiser, M., Eyben, F., Schuller, B., Rigoll, G.: LSTM-modeling of continuous emotions in an audiovisual affect recognition framework. Image Vis. Comput. **31**(2), 153–163 (2013)

Modelling User Experience
in Human-Robot Interactions

Kristiina Jokinen[1,2(✉)] and Graham Wilcock[2]

[1] University of Tartu, Tartu, Estonia
[2] University of Helsinki, Helsinki, Finland
kristiina.jokinen@ut.ee, graham.wilcock@helsinki.fi

Abstract. In human-human interaction, the participants' multimodal behaviour has impact on the interaction as a whole, and similarly in spoken human-robot interactions, the interlocutors' multimodal signals seem to correlate with the user's experience and impressions of the interaction. We explored in more detail how some aspects of multimodal behaviour (gazing, facial expressions, body posture) can predict the user's evaluation of the robot's behaviour (Responsiveness, Expressiveness, Interface, Usability, Overall impression). The results indicate that the user's assessment concerning the evaluation categories Interface and Usability, and to some extent the categories Expressiveness and Overall correlate with their behaviour in a statistically significant manner. The work contributes to our understanding of how the interlocutors' engagement and active participation relate to their assessment of the success of communication, and points towards automating evaluation of human-robot interactions.

Keywords: Multimodal human-robot interaction · Evaluation · User experience

1 Introduction

Research on human-human interactions has shown that the interlocutors' multimodal behaviour and emotional state have impact on the interaction as a whole and on how pleasant the experience has been [2, 9]. In human-robot interaction, it can be assumed that the user's engagement in the interaction can also be inferred from the participants' multimodal activity in a similar manner and consequently, be used to estimate the user's experience of the interaction with the robot system.

In our earlier work [13], we studied the user's engagement with a humanoid robot system and focused on their multimodal behaviour which correlates with the interactive system's evaluation categories. The results supported the original hypothesis that by observing the user's multi-modal behaviour and emotional state, as well as the robot's appropriate responses, it was possible to estimate the user's engagement in the interaction and to predict the user's experience of the various aspects of the interaction with the robot system. We now continue this line of research and investigate in more detail how different combinations of the multimodal behaviours (gazing, facial expressions, body posture) can predict the user's experience and evaluation of spoken interaction with respect to evaluation categories such as Responsiveness, Expressiveness, Interface, Usability, and Overall impression.

© Springer International Publishing Switzerland 2015
R. Böck et al. (Eds.): MA3HMI 2014 Workshop, LNAI 8757, pp. 45–56, 2015.
DOI: 10.1007/978-3-319-15557-9_5

The work contributes to multimodal interaction modeling and to our understanding of how the interlocutors' engagement and active participation relate to their assessment of the success of communication. It also contributes to the evaluation methodology of interactive human-robot systems, by emphasizing the communicative experience of the users, and points towards automating evaluation of human-robot interactions. In particular, the study draws on the naturalness of interactions and measures the users' engagement through their multimodal activity rather than focusing solely on task completion and efficient communication of factual information.

The paper is structured as follows. Section 2 gives an overview of related research concerning multimodal evaluation and human-robot interaction. Section 3 describes the data and Sect. 4 presents the experiments and results. Finally, Sect. 5 draws conclusions and describes plans for future work.

2   Multimodal Evaluation

Evaluation of spoken dialogue systems is a complex issue and, as pointed out by [12], multimodality adds a new dimension to it: the full repertoire of the communicative capability of the system. The perceived naturalness of the interaction does not depend only on task-based dialogue strategies, but also on the combined effect of the different modalities that can be exploited in the communication. The evaluation metrics would need to include accuracy and effectiveness of each modality engine separately, but also capture the interdependence between the perceptual categories related to modalities. The evaluation thus requires a holistic approach. Since there is not only one possible mapping between the modalities, tasks and user preferences, a multidimensional evaluation is necessary.

In the evaluation of the multimodal system SmartKom [3], the task-based spoken dialogue system evaluation framework Paradise [19] was extended to cover specific issues concerning multimodality in the three SmartKom scenarios (home, public, mobile). By abstracting over functionally similar modality technologies that can be used in parallel (speech, gesture, and facial recognition) and weighting and relating different modalities that work in cooperation or sequentially (e.g. gesture recognition is easier than speech recognition in more limited domain), the measures took into account the efficiency of each modality as well as synchrony of the modalities. The relations between modalities, tasks, and user preferences were presented in a common attribute-value matrix while kappa-statistic was used to capture variability between different users as well as in one single user when using the system in different situations.

In social robotics, the robots should communicate with humans in a socially correct way. Due to flexible use of various technologies, their communicative capability becomes rich and more natural: the ability to recognize the user's spoken and multimodal utterances is combined with output that includes speech, gesturing and possibly other modalities. Moreover, situated, embodied human-robot interactions resemble interactive situations between two agents, so the evaluation is easily levelled to include properties of natural interaction between humans. As a starting point for metrics for HRI, especially when assessing the performance of human-robot teams, [17] have taken the notion of Situational Awareness [8], which means that the robot needs to understand what is important in the situation. The level of awareness depends on the level of the robot's autonomous behaviour and the role of the human in the situation, but the main issue is how the awareness is communicated to the partner, i.e. how the user gets feedback from the robot's understanding of the situation and actions being undertaken, and vice versa. In spoken dialogue systems [12] this has been an important design principle discussed under the concepts of grounding and feedback. It is also emphasized, however, that the performance of an HRI system is not only based on interaction design: a failure may be due to malfunctioning of the robot's software or sensory system rather than an issue with the user interface. The multidimensional and holistic evaluation requirements discussed above thus also apply to social robotics.

In this paper, we approach evaluation from the point of view of perceived communication capabilities of the robot and by observing the user's holistic behaviour that signals their awareness of the situation. We consider spoken interaction with a Nao robot application, and assume that by measuring the user's multimodal behaviour and emotional state, as well as the robot's appropriate responses, it is possible to predict the user's experience and consequently their evaluation of the various aspects of the interaction with the robot. Previous studies have used speech prosody [14], silence duration [7], gaze [15], and utterance density [5] as measures to estimate the user's activity and engagement in interaction, while models for an artificial agent's multimodal feedback strategy have been proposed e.g. by [11, 16]. In the context of humanoid robots, [4] studied shared attention models to allow the robot to classify perceptual input into stimuli to which it could learn to react. However, none of the studies has directly tried to estimate the user's experience and evaluation categories on the basis of their multi-modal behaviour in order to learn how multimodal correlates can be used to infer the user's evaluation of their interaction with a humanoid robot. In our previous studies [13], we set out to investigate if it is possible to estimate the user's experience of the various aspects of the interaction with the robot system, and how this corresponds to their evaluation of the system. We take this as our current starting point, and extend the study towards a holistic view of communication. We use the combinations of various perceptual correlates of the user's multimodal behaviour (gaze, gesture, body) and study how they indicate the user's awareness of the interaction and can be used as a basis for feedback in joint communication.

3 Data

Our corpus of *eNTERFACE-2012 Nao-Human Interaction Data* contains videos of human-robot spoken interactions using the WikiTalk system [20]. The robot uses gestures, nods, and other multimodal signals to give expressive presentations of requested spoken information [6, 10], and the corpus was systematically collected to evaluate three slightly different versions of the system [1]. Twelve users interacted with the system, resulting in a corpus of $12 \times 3 = 36$ interactions. The corpus is available for research purposes. Figure 1 shows screenshots from some of the videos.

The corpus was annotated with Elan [22] concerning multimodal behaviours which are generally used to signal comprehension of the message or to display affective state.

Fig. 1. Users interacting with the Nao robot.

Table 1 lists the five annotation categories with the associated binary features. These include the user's gaze (focus of attention), overt facial expressions, body movement, and an approximation of the user's emotional state. The robot's behaviour was annotated with respect to its perceived appropriateness in the situation, loosely following the appropriateness annotation in [18]. Annotations were made simultaneously by four annotators, and their pair-wise kappa ranged between 0.32 for facial expressions to 0.82 on body movement.

In the experiments we only took into account features that had frequency of at least nine in the corpus. It is interesting that there were not enough examples of the user's hand gestures (although the annotation scheme also contained tags for this), so the hand gesture category was dropped from the experiments. Further analysis showed that the user's hand gestures were not related to their natural communicative behaviour, but mostly to controlling the robot's behaviour (e.g. tap on the head to stop it talking in emergency situation), i.e. induced by the interface rather than by spontaneous reaction.

Table 1. Annotation categories (n = 5) and their features (n = 16) used in the experiments.

Annotation category	Number of features	Example features
User gaze	3	toRobot, toInstructor, toBackground
User emotional expression	6	amused, disappointed, interested, sad, satisfied, uncertain
User body engagement	1	leansTowardsRobot
User facial expression	2	smile, laugh
Robot appropriateness	4	ok, offThePoint, odd, okByChance

After each interaction the users also filled in a questionnaire about their experience of the particular system version. The evaluation categories for the users to assess their experience and various aspects of the robot interaction are given in Table 2. Each of the five evaluation categories consisted of 5–8 evaluative statements, and the users had to score them using a 5-point Likert scale, with 1 denoting total disagreement and 5 total agreement with a particular statement.

The users had also provided their expectations of the robot interaction before the beginning of the evaluation session. This was done by filling in a similar questionnaire

Table 2. Evaluation categories for user experience.

Expressiveness	The robot's lively behaviour and clear and expressive presentation
Responsiveness	The robot's quick and appropriate reaction
Interface	Technical aspects of the speech interface
Usability	The robot's performance in the open-domain conversation task
Overall	General aspects of the interaction design

which asked about their expectations rather than experience. More information about the questionnaires, processing of the ratings, as well as the differences between the users' experience and expectations can be found in [1].

4   Results

Following our previous studies [13], we used Weka [21] to run classification algorithms to estimate how well the annotation features of a particular interaction predict the user's evaluation score for that interaction.

The interaction is represented by an *interaction instance vector* which consists of elements denoting the 16 multimodal annotation features for the interaction listed in Table 1. The class variable to be predicted is selected from the five evaluation categories in Table 2. The values of an instance vector are independent numeric variables corresponding to the frequencies of the annotation features in the particular interaction, normalized with respect to the length of the interaction in seconds. The class element is formulated as the numeric average of the evaluative statement scores for that evaluation category, given the interaction and the user. For instance, the evaluation of Responsiveness consisted of eight evaluative statements, and the evaluation score for the Responsiveness category is the average of the eight evaluation scores that the user had given for the Responsiveness statements in the questionnaire of the given interaction. When predicting the correlation between multimodal features and the evaluation category, the same interaction instance vector is combined with each of the five evaluation categories separately.

We used Weka's instance filter to discretize the numeric class variables into nominal attributes (5-bin relates to a 5-point Likert scale, but we also experimented with 3-bin), as we wanted to experiment with a classification as well as with a regression model. We experimented with Weka's logistic regression (maximum entropy model) and Support Vector Machine algorithms, but the differences between the two were not statistically significant, so below we report the SVM results only. As for the comparison field, we used percentage correct and the weighted average f-measure. Weka's Zero-R (majority category) was used as a majority baseline. All experiments were conducted via ten-fold cross-validation.

4.1   Predicting User Experience with Multimodal Features

Table 3 shows the SVM results (percent correct and weighted average f-measure) for classifying interaction instances with all the 16 multimodal annotation features into the five evaluation categories (cf. [13]). As can be seen, if we look at the percent-correct values, the multimodal annotation features predict the evaluation category Usability best, and they also work fairly well for Responsiveness and Interface. On the other hand, f-measure brings in Overall and Interface, besides Usability. The differences in the predictions among the categories are not statistically significant, but they support a tendency of the predictive power of the multimodal annotation features focusing on the evaluation categories Usability and Interface, i.e. relating to technical aspects and the robot's interaction capability.

Table 3. SVM classification with 16 multimodal features, following [13]. Standard deviation is in parenthesis.

Evaluation category	Percent correct	Weighted average F-measure
Expressiveness	39.00 (21.25)	0.29 (0.20)
Responsiveness	**40.58 (15.43)**	0.27 (0.13)
Interface	**40.42 (20.22)**	**0.30 (0.22)**
Usability	**42.92 (21.76)**	**0.33 (0.22)**
Overall	37.50 (22.71)	**0.30 (0.21)**

We also used Weka's *CfsSubsetEval* attribute selection algorithm with the best first search strategy (greedy hill-climbing with backtracking) to select a subset of the best predictive features. The selection is based on considering the predictive ability of each feature together with the mutual redundancy of the features, and preferred subsets are those that correlate highly with the class but have low inter-correlation. Using ten-fold cross-validation, the algorithm selects the best feature set for each evaluation category, shown in Table 4.

Table 4. Best features for the evaluation categories, from [13].

Evaluation category	Best features selected
Expressiveness (5)	gazedParticipantInstructor, emotionalExpression-Amused, emotionalExpression-Disappointed, emotionalExpression-Satisfied, appropriateness-odd
Responsiveness (5)	gazedParticipantInstructor, emotionalExpression-Amused, emotionalExpression-Disappointed, emotionalExpression-Sad, emotionalExpression-Satisfied
Interface (6)	emotionalExpression-Amused, emotionalExpression-Disappointed, emotionalExpression-Satisfied, appropriateness-okByChance, appropriateness-offThePoint, appropriateness-odd
Usability (5)	gazedParticipantInstructor, emotionalExpression-Amused, emotionalExpression-Sad, emotionalExpression-Satisfied, appropriateness-okByChance
Overall (8)	gazedParticipantInstructor, emotionalExpression-Amused, emotionalExpression-Disappointed, emotionalExpression-Sad, appropriateness-OK, appropriateness-odd, facialExpression-smile, facialExpression-laugh

Using the selected best features for a new SVM classification, we get the results in Table 5. As expected, accuracy is better than using the whole set of features, except for Responsiveness, for which the accuracy almost halves. Unlike the other evaluation categories, the robot's appropriate reaction seems to be difficult to associate with any specific multimodal feature set, but all the annotated features seem important in its prediction. It is interesting that none of the features that are specifically used to annotate the robot's perceived appropriateness (ok, offThePoint, odd, okByChance) are among the best features for predicting Responsiveness; apparently the outside view of the robot's appropriate behavior as annotated in the corpus does not directly translate to the user's own experience and inside view of the behavior as described by the user's evaluation scores.

Of the other categories, Usability is still predicted with the highest accuracy. However, the pruning of the features causes Expressiveness to be predicted significantly better than with the full feature set. This may be due to the bias in the selected best features which seem to favour gazing and emotional expression which are important signals in expressive behaviour. We can, however, conclude that multimodal annotation features function as important parameters in interaction evaluation, lending support for the original hypothesis that the user's multimodal behaviour predicts their experience of the interaction with the system.

Table 5. SVM classification on the best feature set for each evaluation category (standard deviation in parenthesis), from [13].

Evaluation category	Percent correct	Weighted average F-measure
Expressiveness	**53.25 (15.84)**	**0.41 (0.19)**
Responsiveness	23.58 (18.84)	0.17 (0.16)
Interface	45.67 (11.75)	0.31 (0.10)
Usability	**53.08 (22.49)**	**0.44 (0.26)**
Overall	49.92 (19.08)	0.40 (0.20)

4.2 Combination of Features for Predicting the Evaluation

To study the above hypothesis in more detail, we ask which annotation features and combinations of features provide important feedback to the participants concerning the partner's interest, emotions, awareness, and level of understanding. These features can then also function as signals that automatic agents should learn to observe and use to predict the user's interaction engagement. Based on the best predicting features in Table 4, we selected the features describing gaze, perceived emotional expression, and appropriateness as the main modality features. We also formed several linguistically motivated combinations of the multimodal features listed in Table 1, to investigate if the features form patterns that bear predictive correlations with the five evaluation categories.

Table 6 (next page) presents the best classification results in the following five cases: single annotation features of gaze, emotional expression, and appropriateness only, the combination of gaze, body and face features (the observable features for the user behaviour), and the combination of gaze, body, face, and appropriateness (the features that describe dynamic interaction between the observed user behaviour and the perceived appropriateness of robot behaviour).

Table 6. Features as predictors. **Bold-faced** are the best performing predictors, and bold-faced capitalized features mark significant differences compared with *italic* capitalized features within an evaluation category (p < 0.05).

Evaluation category	Annotation feature	Percent correct	Weighted average F-measure
Overall	gaze	26.50 (16.60)	0.16 (0.14)
	EMOTION	*25.92 (17.12)*	*0.16 (0.14)*
	appropriate	32.00 (19.34)	0.22 (0.18)
	GAZE-BODY-FACE	**39.58 (21.46)**	**0.30 (0.22)**
	appr-gaze-body-face	39.42 (24.78)	0.32 (0.23)
Usability	gaze	41.67 (16.33)	0.26 (0.17)
	emotion	**44.08 (21.53)**	**0.33 (0.22)**
	appropriate	41.67 (16.33)	0.27 (0.17)
	gaze-body-face	41.00 (16.74)	0.28 (0.17)
	appr-gaze-body-face	39.50 (17.99)	0.28 (0.17)
Expressiveness	*GAZE*	*30.33 (17.23)*	*0.19 (0.16)*
	EMOTION	**43.83 (21.96)**	**0.32 (0.22)**
	APPROPRIATE	**45.67 (19.12)**	**0.32 (0.21)**
	gaze-body-face	39.25 (20.56)	0.28 (0.20)
	appr-gaze-body-face	39.83 (22.68)	0.29 (0.22)
Responsiveness	**gaze**	**45.83 (11.39)**	**0.30 (0.12)**
	emotion	43.50 (13.43)	0.29 (0.12)
	appropriate	**45.83 (11.39)**	**0.30 (0.12)**
	gaze-body-face	45.33 (11.74)	0.29 (0.12)
	appr-gaze-body-face	43.25 (13.54)	0.28 (0.12)
Interface	*GAZE*	*25.42 (14.86)*	*0.14 (0.11)*
	emotion	33.50 (17.77)	0.22 (0.18)
	APPROPRIATE	**40.83 (18.56)**	**0.29 (0.20)**
	GAZE-BODY-FACE	*21.42 (13.88)*	*0.11 (0.09)*
	appr-gaze-body-face	36.75 (19.21)	0.26 (0.20)

Comparing the predictive power of annotation features across the five evaluation categories, the tested combinations of multimodal features do not necessarily do better than the features for single modalities. An exception is the Overall evaluation category, for which the combination features perform significantly better than any single modality feature set, thus conforming to the hypothesis that the user's overall experience of the robot is affected by all the multimodal features together. However, the linguistically based combinations do not reach the same level of accuracy as the pruned feature sets listed in Table 5, but they do, nevertheless, perform better than a classification with all the original features in Table 3, thus supporting the bias based on linguistically meaningful combinations over a flat use of all perceived features.

Of the tested feature combinations, the robot's perceived appropriateness was the best predicting feature for Expressiveness and Interface, and it did well for Responsiveness, Overall, and Usability, too. The user's emotional expression features predict significantly best for Expresiveness, and well also for Responsiveness and Usability compared with Interface or Overall categories. The user's gaze predicts significantly well for Responsiveness and Usability compared with Interface or Overall categories. This can be considered natural, since gaze indicates the agent's focus of attention and orientation towards the partner rather than general properties of speech interface or interaction design. In our experiments, gaze is significantly the worst predictor for Expressiveness, although this does not mean that it would be so in general. Our gaze annotations did not mark possible emotional signaling of eye-gaze, but only the focus and orientation of the user's attention, so we can only conclude that these two particular functions of eye-gaze cannot be used to predict Expressiveness.

We also compared the selected feature-sets pair-wise within each of the five evaluation categories, on their percentage correct values and weighted average f-measure values using Weka's experimental environment with two-tailed Student's t-test. Table 6 shows visually the statistically significant differences between the highest (bold-faced) and the lowest (italics) accuracy values within each evaluation category on the confidence level 0.05.

For instance, to predict Expressiveness, the features related to the robot's appropriate response and the user's emotional state are significantly better predictors than gaze features alone. The result seems natural when considering the user's experience of the *expressiveness* of the interaction: as discussed above, observing where the user's focus of attention (gaze) is directed is not as relevant as the perceived behaviour of the robot, or the user's own emotional state. The appropriateness and emotional state features also predict better than the two combination features, but the difference here is not statistically significant.

The robot's appropriate responses were better predictors also for the category Interface, compared with the features related to the user's gaze, or the combination of gaze with body movements and facial expressions. Considering the category Overall, appropriateness of robot responses and the user's gaze, body movement and facial expressions (the dynamic interaction features) together predict the category better than the perceived emotional state of the user. This seems like an acceptable conclusion since the Overall category concerns interaction in general.

As for the categories Usability and Responsiveness, the situation is quite the opposite. All the features and feature combinations seem to predict the categories in a similar manner, i.e. no feature stands out as a significantly powerful indicator of these evaluation categories. Although for Usability, the user's perceived emotional state predicts fairly high, the difference is not statistically significant if the prediction is compared with the predictions produced by the other feature combinations. Responsiveness, on the other hand, has fairly even predictions with all the feature combinations, and it is particularly interesting that the objective views of the robot's behaviour (annotations for appropriateness) do not seem to have any strong correlation with the user's perception of the robot's quick and appropriate actions (as measured through the evaluation category). Either the user's perception does not correlate with the objective observations of the robot's behaviour, or the user's evaluation of the robot's appropriate actions does not depend on how appropriate the actions seem to be. This opens up interesting discussions related to the subjective and objective analysis of the interaction, as seen by an inside participant vs. an outside observer: the participant's experience of an interaction does not necessarily follow the outside observations of what seems to happens in the situation.

5 Conclusions

We have studied the user's multimodal behaviour and its impact on their evaluation of interaction in spoken human-robot interactive situations. The results show how the annotation parameters of multimodal behaviour can predict the user's experience and impressions of the success of the speech-based human-robot interactions, and we found statistically significant correlations between the users' multimodal activity and their evaluation of the robot application.

The work contributes to our understanding of how the interlocutors' engagement in a communicative situation is related to their active participation in the interaction. Our research also provides a preliminary set of multimodal features which have an impact on communication and, consequently, can be used to predict the user's evaluation of an interactive application. The data used in our studies may not provide an exhaustive feature set, but the results encourage us to go further to fully establish the hypothesis of the use of multimodal behaviour in measuring interaction experience.

It is clear that human engagement, interest, and attention in interactive situations are complex issues, and the number of multimodal annotation features needed for accurate description is high. Future work will concern experimenting with larger interaction data and refining the annotation features and feature combinations. An interesting topic in this respect is also to investigate further the relation between subjective experience and objective description of the interactive situation.

Another future line of research concerns the use automatic or semi-automatic methods to detect the various multimodal features from the video and speech signals, and to calculate correlations between multimodal activity and the user's engagement in the interaction. It is possible to upload such a model into the robot's behaviour library and use it as an independent module that provides predictions of the user's active engagement in the interaction. From the point of view of interactive system design, such a model can be used to enhance the robot's interpretation and anticipation of the human behaviour in interactive situations, and to study the combined effect of the user's verbal and non-verbal signaling of their engagement and experience of the interaction.

Acknowledgements. We would like to thank all the participants as well as the annotators of the video files.

References

1. Anastasiou, D., Jokinen, K., Wilcock, G.: Evaluation of WikiTalk – user studies of human-robot interaction. In: Kurosu, M. (ed.) HCII/HCI 2013, Part IV. LNCS, vol. 8007, pp. 32–42. Springer, Heidelberg (2013)
2. Bavelas, J.B., Black, A., Lemery, C.R., Mullett, J.: I show how you feel: motor mimicry as a communicative act. J. Pers. Soc. Psychol. **50**(2), 322–329 (1986)
3. Beringer, N., Kartal, U., Louka, K., Schiel, F., Türk, U.: PROMISE: a procedure for multimodal interactive system evaluation. In: Proceedings of the Workshop Multimodal Resources and Multimodal Systems Evaluation, Las Palmas (2002)

4. Breazeal, C., Scassellati, B.: A context-dependent attention system for a social robot. In: Proceedings of the 16th International Joint Conference in Artificial Intelligence (IJCAI 1999), Stockholm, pp. 1146–1151 (1999)
5. Campbell, N., Scherer, S.: Comparing measures of synchrony and alignment in dialogue speech timing with respect to turn-taking activity. In: Proceedings of Interspeech 2010, Makuhari (2010)
6. Csapo, A., Gilmartin, E., Grizou, J., Han, J., Meena, R., Anastasiou, D., Jokinen, K., Wilcock, G.: Multimodal conversational interaction with a humanoid robot. In: Proceedings of 3rd IEEE International Conference on Cognitive Infocommunications (CogInfoCom 2012), Kosice, pp. 667–672 (2012)
7. Edlund, J., Heldner, M., Hirschberg, J.: Pause and gap length in face-to-face interaction. In: Proceedings of Interspeech 2009, Brighton (2009)
8. Endsley, M.R.: Theoretical underpinnings of situation awareness: a critical review. In: Endsley, M.R., Garland, D.J. (eds.) Situation Awareness Analysis and Measurement. LEA, Mahwah (2000)
9. Goodwin, C.: Action and embodiment within situated human interaction. J. Pragmat. **32**, 1489–1522 (2000)
10. Han, J., Campbell, N., Jokinen, K., Wilcock, G.: Investigating the use of non-verbal cues in human-robot interaction with a Nao robot. In: Proceedings of 3rd IEEE International Conference on Cognitive Infocommunications (CogInfoCom 2012), Kosice, pp. 679–683 (2012)
11. Ishii, R., Nakano, Y., Nishida, T.: Gaze awareness in conversational agents: Estimating a user's conversational engagement from eye gaze. ACM Trans. Interact. Intell. Syst. **3**(2), 11:1–11:25 (2013)
12. Jokinen, K., McTear, M.: Spoken Dialogue Systems. Morgan and Claypool, San Rafael (2009)
13. Jokinen, K., Wilcock, G.: User experience in human-robot interactions. In: Schatz, R., Hossfeld, T. (eds.) Proceedings of the Fourth Workshop on Perceptual Quality of Systems (PQS 2013), FTW-TECHREPORT-128, FTW, Vienna, Austria (2013)
14. Levitan, R., Gravano, A., Hirschberg, J.: Entrainment in speech preceding backchannels. In: Proceedings of ACL 2011, pp. 113–117 (2011)
15. Levitski, A., Radun, J., Jokinen, K.: Visual interaction and conversational activity. In: Proceedings of the 4th Workshop on Eye Gaze in Intelligent Human Machine Interaction: Eye Gaze and Multimodality, at the 14th ACM International Conference on Multimodal Interaction (ICMI 2012), Santa Monica, California, USA (2012)
16. Nakano, Y., Reinstein, G., Stocky, T., Cassell, J.: Towards a model of face-to-face grounding. In: Proceedings of the 41st Annual Meeting on Association for Computational Linguistics, vol. 1, pp. 553–561 (2003)
17. Steinfeld, A., Fong, T., Kaber, D., Scholtz, J., Schultz, A., Goodrich, M.: Common metrics for human-robot interaction. In: 2006 Human-Robot Interaction Conference (2006)
18. Traum, D., Robinson, S., Stephan, J.: Evaluation of multi-party virtual reality dialogue interaction. In: Proceedings of Fourth International Conference on Language Resources and Evaluation (LREC 2004), Lisbon, pp. 1699–1702 (2004)
19. Walker, M., Litman, D., Kamm, C., Abella, A.: PARADISE: a framework for evaluating spoken dialogue agents. In: Proceedings of the 35th Annual Meeting of the Association for Computational Linguistics, Madrid (1997)
20. Wilcock, G.: WikiTalk: a spoken Wikipedia-based open-domain knowledge access system. In: Proceedings of the COLING 2012 Workshop on Question Answering in Complex Domains, Mumbai, India, pp. 57–69 (2012)

21. Witten, I., Frank, E., Hall, M.: Data Mining: Practical Machine Learning Tools and Techniques, 3rd edn. Morgan Kaufmann, San Francisco (2011)
22. Wittenburg, P., Brugman, H., Russel, A., Klassmann, A., Sloetjes, H.: ELAN: a professional framework for multimodality research. In: Proceedings of the Fifth International Conference on Language Resources and Evaluation (LREC 2006), pp. 1556–1559 (2006)

Disposition Recognition from Spontaneous Speech Towards a Combination with Co-speech Gestures

Ronald Böck[1]([⊠]), Kirsten Bergmann[2], and Petra Jaecks[3]

[1] Faculty of Electrical Engineering and Information Technology,
Otto von Guericke University, P.O. Box 4120, 39016 Magdeburg, Germany
ronald.boeck@ovgu.de
[2] Faculty of Technology, Bielefeld University,
P.O. Box 100 131, 33501 Bielefeld, Germany
kirsten.bergmann@uni-bielefeld.de
[3] Faculty of Linguistics and Literary Studies, Bielefeld University,
P.O. Box 100 131, 33501 Bielefeld, Germany
petra.jaecks@uni-bielefeld.de
http://www.cogsy.de

Abstract. Speech as well as co-speech gestures are an integral part of human communicative behaviour. Furthermore, the way how these modalities influence each other and finally, reflect a speaker's dispositional state is an important aspect of research in Human-Machine-Interaction. So far, just little is known, however, about the simultaneous investigation of both modalities. The EmoGest corpus is a novel data set addressing how emotions or dispositions manifest themselves in co-speech gestures. Participants were primed to be happy, neutral, or sad and afterwards, explain tangram figures to an experimenter. We employed this corpus to conduct disposition recognition from speech data as an evaluation of emotion priming. For the analysis, we based the classification on meaningful features already successfully applied in emotion recognition. In disposition recognition from speech, we achieved remarkable classification accuracy. These results provide the basis for a detailed disposition-related analyses of gestural behaviour, also in combination with speech. In general, the necessity of multimodal investigations of disposition is indicated which then will be heading towards an improvement of overall performance.

Keywords: Human-machine-interaction · Disposition recognition from speech · Co-speech gestures · Naturalistic human-machine-interaction

1 Introduction

The way human beings communicate with technical systems in a sense of Human-Maschine-Interaction (HMI) changed drastically in the last years [7]. Especially, the usage of modalities like speech, video, etc. influences the course of interaction

© Springer International Publishing Switzerland 2015
R. Böck et al. (Eds.): MA3HMI 2014 Workshop, LNAI 8757, pp. 57–66, 2015.
DOI: 10.1007/978-3-319-15557-9_6

more and more towards naturalistic communication. Such additional modalities allow further systems which can recognise and interpret information sources like facial expressions, gestures, and various information from speech [34]. Nevertheless, the ultimate goal that HMI is similar or equal to a Human-Human-Interaction (HHI) is still not reached. Considering the mentioned sources of information, speech and gestures are an integral part of humans' communication. Especially, the combination of both sources could lead to a better understanding of the interaction between a user and a system. Co-speech gestures that accompany speech are very closely linked to the semantic content of the speech that they are related to, in both form and timing. Speech and gesture together comprise an utterance and both together externalise thought. They are believed to emerge from the same underlying cognitive representation and to be governed, at least in parts, by the same cognitive processes [13,18]. Furthermore, the dispositional state of a user influences the way of interaction (cf. e.g. [4,28]). Therefore, we investigate the dispositional state of a user in an interaction where additionally co-speech gestures were intended. At the moment, the question if and how dispositional reactions influence the gesturing behaviour of a user is an emerging topic of research (cf. [8,14]). The term disposition describes the characteristics and behaviour of a user in a broader sense than the term emotion. For this, it includes besides emotions also aspects of moods and more subtle reactions on certain situations (cf. [4,9,28]).

In this paper, we investigate the dispositional state of the subjects recorded in the EmoGest corpus [2], collected at the University Bielefeld, based on speech data. The data set, generally, allows combined analyses of speech and co-speech gestures in a naturalistic interaction. Naturalistic means that on the one hand, the subjects were no actors playing a certain disposition and on the other hand, no pre-defined wordings, gestures, or dispositions (the participants were not told to behave in a specific way) have been given to the subjects. Nevertheless, the participants were musically primed to be in a certain disposition, namely happy or sad [2].

With these analyses we pursued two goals: (i) Investigate the dispositional state of the subjects from speech in this naturalistic corpus. (ii) Due to the quite good recognition results in terms of disposition recognition from speech (cf. e.g. [23,25,29]) and the discriminative power of spectral and prosodic features extracted from speech (cf. e.g. [1,5,31]), the methods of disposition recognition were applied to assure that the dispositional priming of the subjects has worked. Therefore, this paper provides a kind of ground truth for future analysis of co-speech gestures on the EmoGest corpus which leads toward a combination of speech and gestures in the analysis of user behaviour in HMI. To be specific, this paper presents no results on a combination of speech and co-speech gestures. It rather lays foundations to establish such a combination in future work.

The remaining paper is organised as follows: In Sect. 2, the EmoGest corpus is briefly introduced. The experimental setup in terms of utilised features and classifiers is described in Sect. 3. Section 4 presents the achieved classification results on the data set. Finally, we come back to the goals of this paper while concluding our findings.

2   Data Set

The corpus was set up based on a linguistic experiment which consisted of two experimental phases. In the first phase participants underwent a musical emotion induction procedure. 32 participants were randomly assigned to one of three experimental conditions (happy, neutral, and sad) and listened to an audio file of about 3 min length each presenting musical pieces that differed in emotional value (cf. [10, 12] for a description and statistics of the stimuli). Subsequently, they filled out two self-rating questionnaires to evaluate the effect of musical emotion induction. To make sure, that the induced emotion was still present when participants entered the second experimental phase, they listened to the same audio file once again. Thereafter, they fulfilled a gesture-eliciting task in dialogical interaction with a confederate partner which consisted of alternating tangram description to be matched by the partner. The primary data of the corpus consists of audio and HD video recordings of these interactions as well as Kinect data. For the videotape three synchronized camera views were recorded. In total, the corpus provides roughly 12 h of multimodal material. For this, the corpus fits well for our analyses, namely, the recognition of dispositional speech in a naturalistic interaction and the classification of co-speech gestures (not matter of this paper), separately. Further, due to the availability of both modalities (speech and gesture), in future work a combination of these can be applied for a comprehensive analysis of user characteristics in HHI and HMI.

The three experimental groups were comparable in handedness according to the Edinburgh handedness inventory [20] (27 right, 4 left, 1 ambidextrous; $\chi^2 = 2.651$, $p = 0.618$) and gender distribution ($\chi^2 = 3.269$, $p = 0.195$). They did not differ in age (20–41 years, $\chi^2 = 2.327$, $p = 0.312$) or years of education (13–25 years, $\chi^2 = 1.420$, $p = 0.492$). In addition to the recordings, several personality questionnaires were conducted. The three different condition groups were not different in personality traits (BFI-K, [22]; e.g. extraversion: $\chi^2 = 4.409$, $p = 0.110$), actual mood (UWIST, [16]; $\chi^2 = 0.384$, $p = 0.825$) or empathy (SPF/IRI, [21]; $\chi^2 = 0.670$, $p = 0.715$).

To evaluate the priming effect of the musical emotion induction, two different tests were applied. After listening to the music, the groups differed in their feelings of 'joyful activation', 'wonder', 'power', 'tension', 'sadness' (GEM Scale, [35]) as well as valence and activity (dimensional model, [10]). For example, 'joyful activation' is rated significantly higher in the happy condition ($\chi^2 = 16.474$, $p < .000$) providing evidence for a relevant emotional priming effect. Therefore, we argue that it is scientifically sound to compare the three condition groups in further analyses.

In our experiments, according to the dispositional state of the subject, we concentrated on a subset of the EmoGest corpus, namely those participants who were emotionally primed to be in a happy or a sad disposition. Therefore, utterances of 18 subjects (equally distributed to the two dispositions) were analysed in a Leave-One-Speaker-Out (LOSO) manner. To ensure that the priming is still valid only the first 5 min of the interaction were utilised, resulting in 1023 utterances in total. In LOSO the whole data material is used for training except those speech samples of a certain speaker. Whose utterances are used for testing purpose only. The finally presented results in this paper are the recall values averaged over all LOSO runs.

3 Experimental Setup

3.1 Features

Over the past years, two main tendencies were established in terms of feature selection. At first, researchers rely on pure spectral and prosodic features extracted from given speech. The other idea is to use functionals in addition to pure, signal based features. In some cases, both approaches are combined (cf. [25]). In this paper, we pursue the first approach and relied on features extracted frame-wise for each utterance.

Table 1. The two feature sets (with total number of features) used in the experiments with the corresponding applied features.

Feature set	Number	Applied features
MFCC_0_D_A_F_B_I_J_P	48	MFCC_0_D_A, Formants 1–3, Bandwidths, Intensity, Jitter, Pitch
MFCC_0_D_A	39	MFCC, Zeroth Cepstral Coefficient, Delta, Acceleration

According to these considerations, we defined two feature sets (cf. Table 1): The first set contains of Mel-Frequency Cepstral Coefficients (MFCC) 1 to 12 as well as the Zeroth Cepstral Coefficient with corresponding Delta and Acceleration values each. In addition, we accompanied formants 1 to 3, the corresponding bandwidths, intensity, jitter, and pitch. The second feature collection is a subset of the first and is focussed on spectral features only, namely MFCC as well as the Zeroth Cepstral Coefficient with corresponding Delta and Acceleration values (cf. MFCC_0_D_A in Table 1). Both feature sets are recently heavily applied in the research community (cf. e.g. [1, 23–25, 29–31]). Furthermore, they are also used in recognition of spontaneous or naturalistic disposition recognition from speech (cf. e.g. [3, 4, 26, 29]).

For the feature extraction we used two tools, namely, the Hidden Markov Toolkit (HTK) of the University Cambridge [33] and Praat [6]. Both tools were applied frame-wise on each utterance. In general, if windowing is necessary for the corresponding feature extraction a Hamming window with a length of 25 ms is utilised. Furthermore, the window shift is specified to 10 ms. These parameters are widely used in processing of speech signals as well as in disposition recognition from speech (cf. [23, 25]). To generate the first feature set (cf. Table 1) spectral and prosodic values were concatenated applying the Matlab function `writehtk` which handles any type of features and generates suitable files to be used in HTK. `writehtk` is part of the Voicebox Toolbox provided by Kamil Wojcicki [32].

3.2 Classification Method

In disposition recognition from speech the classification is based on a time-continuous signal. Therefore, an appropriate method should cover the characteristics of such input. Usually, this is possible with so-called Hidden Markov Models (HMMs). The temporal evolution of the signal is modelled by transition probabilities indicating a transition from one state to another. The possibility to stay in a certain state is handled by self-loops. Therefore, this type of classifier is a common approach in the community (cf. [19, 24, 25]). Based on this idea (depending on the point of view also the other way around), so-called Gaussian Mixture Models (GMMs) are generated. They are constructed as a one state HMM modelling the characteristics of a dispositional utterance by a combination of several Gaussian distributions. This method is an approach to handle the overall speech characteristic rather than the temporal evolution. It is applied, for instance, in [3, 23, 29]. In our experiments, the different training and test runs vary in terms of mixture numbers. Nevertheless, the training procedure remains the same for all runs: Each GMM is generated as a one state model and the cumulative mixture are trained for 5 iterations (cf. [5]).

For validation of the models, we applied the LOSO strategy as introduced in Sect. 2.

4 Experimental Results

The current work continues the preliminary study presented in [2]. Therefore, we applied the described methods (cf. Sect. 3) to the full EmoGest corpus (cf. Sect. 2) in the sense of dispositionally primed participants. In particular, we used the utterances spoken by the subject in the first 5 min of each interaction since for this, we can assume that the given priming is still valid. Afterwards, several side-effects may corrupt the priming and thus, influence the subject's disposition. In particular, as already introduced in Sect. 2, two main classes are given by design of the corpus, namely happy and sad, which were also used in the disposition recognition from speech.

Based on the extracted two feature sets given in Table 1, we trained GMMs utilising HTK [33]. Notice that for each class a single GMM was generated and a final decision was established by passing through the models using the Viterbi algorithm. In Table 2 we present the results concentrating on a few numbers of mixtures. Nevertheless, we evaluate also GMM settings with various numbers of mixtures – in intermediate ranges –, but the achieved results were similar to those given in Table 2. Especially, the classifiers which used 9, 81, and 120 Gaussian mixtures gained the best results with slight numerical differences. These parameters are already well-known in the disposition recognition from speech since they are used in the context of other corpora as well. In particular, they are found suitable to deal with dispositions shown in spontaneous interactions. The authors in [3] show that GMMs with 9 mixture components can be used to preselect sequences in the audio stream which are meaningful for further facial expressions' investigations. In [23] it is discussed that 81 Gaussian mixtures are a good parameter estimation for a broad range of naturalistic data sets. Based on this observation, the authors of [27] as well as [29] conclude that for an optimal number of mixtures two maxima are existing. They have shown that the second maximum is located in the neighbourhood of 120 mixtures. occurrencerecognition results are independent from the applied features. Nevertheless, depending on the utilised corpus and feature set they are less pronounced.

Having these considerations in mind, we see from Table 2 that the achieved results have also these two maxima. Again, the validation is based on a LOSO strategy. For this, the ability to identify dispositions independent from a certain user can be shown. In particular, the classifiers reach remarkable results on the full feature set (i.e., MFCC_0_D_A_F_B_I_J_P) of 0.785 recall (cf. Table 2). With 120 Gaussian mixtures the variance has also its minimum. The same results are mirrored for the smaller feature set which just contains spectral features.

Table 2. Experimental results for the two features sets (cf. Table 1) using GMMs with different numbers of mixtures (#mix). The two class recognition results are given in terms of recall with corresponding variance.

Feature set	#mix	Recall	Variance
MFCC_0_D_A_F_B_I_J_P	9	0.755	0.324
	81	0.782	0.327
	120	0.785	0.322
MFCC_0_D_A	9	0.822	0.375
	81	0.826	0.380
	120	0.822	0.375

Analysing the results of the two feature sets separately, we determine that the feature set based on spectral features outperforms the combined one. The recall values are more than 4 % higher absolute staying with the same range of variance. This might tend to the conclusion that spectral features can better cover or distinguish the two dispositions happy and sad. Additional information from prosodic features may confuse the classifier since these have not the discriminative power for the two dispositions on this corpus. This leads to the discussion which features are the most meaningful ones for dispositions. As Schuller et al. already state in [25], usually, feature sets are highly dependent on the observed corpus. In general, investigations on proper features are an emerging topic in the community and thus, will be also under consideration in our future research.

In general, a baseline for a two-class recognition task would be pure guessing. This leaves us with an expected recall of 0.5. For the sake of a more satisfying comparison, the achieved two class results are ranked against published findings on other primed and naturalistic corpora, namely eNTERFACE (primed, [15]), Vera-am-Mittag (VAM, naturalistic, [11]), and Sensitive Artificial Listener (SAL, naturalistic, [17]). Those findings were achieved with GMMs using 6552 features [23] and are given in Table 3. We just considered the arousal dimension for two reasons: (i) For this, a two class problem is defined, namely high and

Table 3. Comparable results using GMMs and 6552 feature using primed and naturalistic corpora (according to arousal values of Table 6 in [23]). The two class recognition results are given in terms of recall (no variance values are given in [23]).

Corpus	Recall
eNTERFACE	0.749
VAM	0.765
SAL	0.612

low arousal, and (ii) the dispositions in the EmoGest – happy and sad – can also be distinguished in the arousal dimension. It can be assumed that happy is related to high arousal whereas sad tends towards low arousal. Comparing our achievements (cf. Table 2) to those in Table 3, we can state that we obtained quite similar results. Besides, in our experiments we used a lower amount of features.

5   Conclusion and Outlook

The issue of disposition recognition from various modalities and sources is a topic which is heavily investigated in the context of HMI. As we already discussed, an extensive investigation and assessment of dispositional behaviour can only be achieved if different modalities are analysed in parallel (cf. e.g. [34]). Given this opportunity the several information sources support each other in the automatic assessment of dispositions. On the other hand, for each modality suitable classifiers and feature sets have to be identified.

This paper investigated the disposition recognition from spontaneous speech on a naturalistic corpus, namely EmoGest [2]. The subjects were musically primed to be either in a happy or a sad dispositional state. Afterwards, they were asked be describe various objects, they have seen in a virtual reality, using speech and co-speech gestures. It can be assumed that the disposition of the user is reflected in speech and in gestures [13,18]. The recognition from speech is already under heavy investigation (cf. e.g. [24–26]) whereas the co-speech gesture analyses are still at the beginning.

Using GMMs and spectral as well as prosodic features, we achieved remarkable results in the classification of the two primed dispositions. With a combined feature set we obtained 0.785 recall which is 2 % absolute better than results achieved on other naturalistic corpora at its best (cf. Tables 2 and 3). Concentrating on spectral features only, we could improve the recognition performance by roughly 4 % absolute, having almost similar variance values. Again, this shows the high flexibility of spectral features in the handling of spoken characteristics (cf. e.g. [5]).

The second result of the paper is the implicit proving of the priming. As we introduced in Sect. 1, we are interested in a kind of ground truth for the analysis of the corpus in terms of co-speech gestures. Due the good performance values of the disposition recognition from speech (cf. Table 2) we can conclude two facts: (i) The recognition from speech can be used as a ground truth, that means, as a kind of automatic annotation for co-speech gestures (similar to the idea presented in [3]). (ii) The priming was implicitly proved by the automatic disposition recognition from speech, especially, since the results were achieved in a LOSO manner. In particular, while analysing results of the subjects separately, we have seen that for certain participants no confusion of the disposition has shown up. This was independent from the disposition itself.

Based on these results, we can further analyse the corpus in a way to identify meaningful, dispositional co-speech gestures in naturalistic conversations. Further, a combination of both modalities will provide a profound understanding of humans dispositions in HMI.

Acknowledgement. We acknowledge continued support by the Transregional Collaborative Research Centre SFB/TRR 62 "Companion-Technology for Cognitive Technical Systems" and the Collaborative Research Centre SFB 673 "Alignment in Communication" both funded by the German Research Foundation (DFG). We also acknowledge the DFG for financing our computing cluster used for parts of this work. Furthermore, we thank Sören Klett and Ingo Siegert for fruitful discussions and support.

References

1. Anagnostopoulos, C.N., Iliou, T., Giannoukos, I.: Features and classifiers for emotion recognition from speech: a survey from 2000 to 2011. Artif. Intell. Rev. **43**(2), 155–177 (2015)
2. Bergmann, K., Böck, R., Jaecks, P.: Emogest: investigating the impact of emotions on spontaneous co-speech gestures. In: Edlund, J., Heylen, D., Paggio, P. (eds.) Proceedings of the Workshop on Multimodal Corpora 2013: Multimodal Corpora: Combining Applied and Basic Research Targets, pp. 13–16. LREC, Reykjavik, Island (2014)
3. Böck, R., Limbrecht-Ecklundt, K., Siegert, I., Walter, S., Wendemuth, A.: Audio-based pre-classification for semi-automatic facial expression coding. In: Kurosu, M. (ed.) HCII/HCI 2013, Part V. LNCS, vol. 8008, pp. 301–309. Springer, Heidelberg (2013)
4. Böck, R.: Multimodal Automatic User Disposition Recognition in Human-Machine Interaction. Ph.D. thesis, Otto von Guericke University Magdeburg (2013)
5. Böck, R., Hübner, D., Wendemuth, A.: Determining optimal signal features and parameters for hmm-based emotion classification. In: Proceedings of the 15th IEEE Mediterranean Electrotechnical Conference, pp. 1586–1590. IEEE, Valletta, Malta (2010)
6. Boersma, P., Weenink, D.: Praat: Doing phonetics by computer (2011)
7. Carroll, J.M.: Human Computer Interaction - brief intro, 2nd edn. The Interaction Design Foundation, Aarhus, Denmark (2013). http://www.interaction-design.org/encyclopedia/human_computer_interaction_hci.html
8. Castellano, G., Villalba, S.D., Camurri, A.: Recognising human emotions from body movement and gesture dynamics. In: Paiva, A.C.R., Prada, R., Picard, R.W. (eds.) ACII 2007. LNCS, vol. 4738, pp. 71–82. Springer, Heidelberg (2007)

9. Chaplin, J.P.: Dictionary of Psychology. Random House Publishing Group, New York (2010)

10. Eerola, T., Vuoskoski, J.K.: A comparison of the discrete and dimensional models of emotion in music. Psychol. Music **39**, 18–49 (2011)

11. Grimm, M., Kroschel, K., Narayanan, S.: The Vera am Mittag German audiovisual emotional speech database. In: Proceedings of the 2008 IEEE International Conference on Multimedia and Expo, pp. 865–868. IEEE (2008)

12. Hunter, P.G., Schellenberg, E.G., Schimmack, U.: Mixed affective responses to music with conflicting cues. Cogn. Emot. **22**(2), 327–352 (2008)

13. Kendon, A.: Gesture: Visible Action as Utterance. Cambridge University Press, New York (2004)

14. Kipp, M., Martin, J.C.: Gesture and emotion: can basic gestural form features discrminate emotions? In: Cohn, J., Nijholt, A., Pantic, M. (eds.) Proceedings of the International Conference on Affective Computing and Intelligent Interaction (ACII-09). IEEE Press (2009)

15. Martin, O., Kotsia, I., Macq, B., Pitas, I.: The eNTERFACE 2005 audio-visual emotion database. In: Proceedings of the 22nd International Conference on Data Engineering Workshop (2006)

16. Matthews, G., Jones, D., Chamberlain, A.: Refining the measurement of mood: the UWIST mood adjective checklist. Br. J. Psychol. **81**, 17–42 (1990)

17. McKeown, G., Valstar, M., Cowie, R., Pantic, M., Schroder, M.: The SEMAINE database: annotated multimodal records of emotionally colored conversations between a person and a limited agent. IEEE Trans. Affect. Comput. **3**(1), 5–17 (2012)

18. McNeill, D.: Gesture and Thought. Phoenix Poets Series. University of Chicago Press, Chicago (2008)

19. Nwe, T.L., Foo, S.W., De Silva, L.C.: Speech emotion recognition using hidden markov models. Speech Commun. **41**(4), 603–623 (2003)

20. Oldfield, R.C.: The assessment and analysis of handedness: the Edinburgh inventory. Neuropsychologia **9**(1), 97–113 (1971)

21. Paulus, C.: Der Saarbrücker Persönlichkeitsfragebogen (IRI) zur Messung von Empathie. Psychometrische evaluation der deutschen Version des interpersonal reactivity index (the Saarbrücken personality questionnaire (IRI) for measuring empathy: A psychometric evaluation of the German version of the interpersonal reactivity index) (2009)

22. Rammstedt, B., John, O.P.: Kurzversion des big five inventory (BFI-K): Entwicklung und Validierung eines ökonomischen Inventars zur Erfassung der fünf Faktoren der Persönlichkeit. Diagnostika **51**, 195–206 (2005)

23. Schuller, B., Vlasenko, B., Eyben, F., Rigoll, G., Wendemuth, A.: Acoustic emotion recognition: a benchmark comparison of performances. In: Proceedings of the IEEE Automatic Speech Recognition and Understanding Workshop. ASRU 2009, Merano, Italy, pp. 552–557 (2009)

24. Schuller, B., Vlasenko, B., Minguez, R., Rigoll, G., Wendemuth, A.: Comparing one and two-stage acoustic modeling in the recognition of emotion in speech. In: 2007 IEEE Workshop on Automatic Speech Recognition and Understanding (ASRU), pp. 596–600 (2007)

25. Schuller, B., Batliner, A., Steidl, S., Seppi, D.: Recognising realistic emotions and affect in speech: state of the art and lessons learnt from the first challenge. Speech Commun. **53**(9–10), 1062–1087 (2011)

26. Siegert, I., Haase, M., Prylipko, D., Wendemuth, A.: Discourse particles and user characteristics in naturalistic human-computer interaction. In: Kurosu, M. (ed.) HCI 2014, Part II. LNCS, vol. 8511, pp. 492–501. Springer, Heidelberg (2014)

27. Siegert, I., Philippou-Hübner, D., Hartmann, K., Böck, R., Wendemuth, A.: Investigations on speaker group dependent modelling for affect recognition from speech. Cogn. Comput. Special Issue: Model. Emot. Behav. Context **6**(4), 892–913 (2014)

28. Traue, H.C., Ohl, F., Brechmann, A., Schwenker, F., Kessler, H., Limbrecht, K., Hoffman, H., Scherer, S., Kotzyba, M., Scheck, A., Walter, S.: A framework for emotions and dispositions in man-companion interaction. In: Rojc, M., Campbell, N. (eds.) Converbal Synchrony in Human-Machine Interaction, pp. 98–140. CRC Press, Boca Raton (2013)

29. Vlasenko, B., Prylipko, D., Böck, R., Wendemuth, A.: Modeling phonetic pattern variability in favor of the creation of robust emotion classifiers for real-life applications. Comput. Speech Lang. **28**(2), 483–500 (2014)

30. Vlasenko, B., Philippou-Hübner, D., Prylipko, D., Böck, R., Siegert, I., Wendemuth, A.: Vowels formants analysis allows straightforward detection of high arousal emotions. In: 2011 IEEE International Conference on Multimedia and Expo (ICME) (2011)

31. Vogt, T., André, E.: Comparing feature sets for acted and spontaneous speech in view of automatic emotion recognition. In: IEEE International Conference on Multimedia and Expo 2005, pp. 474–477. IEEE, Amsterdam (2005)

32. Wojcicki, K.: writehtk. In: Voicebox Toolbox (2011). http://www.mathworks.com/matlabcentral/fileexchange/32849-htk-mfcc-matlab/content/mfcc/writehtk.m. Accessed 10 July 2014

33. Young, S., Evermann, G., Gales, M., Hain, T., Kershaw, D., Liu, X., Moore, G., Odell, J., Ollason, D., Povey, D., Valtchev, V., Woodland, P.: The HTK Book, version 3.4. Cambridge University Engineering Department, Cambridge (2009)

34. Zeng, Z., Pantic, M., Roisman, G.I., Huang, T.S.: A survey of affect recognition methods: audio, visual, and spontaneous expressions. IEEE Trans. Pattern Anal. Mach. Intell. **31**(1), 39–58 (2009)

35. Zentner, M., Grandjean, D., Scherer, K.: Emotions evoked by the sound of music: characterization, classification, and measurement. Emotion **8**(4), 494–521 (2008)

Dialogs and Speech Recognition

ASR Independent Hybrid Recurrent Neural Network Based Error Correction for Dialog System Applications

Junhwi Choi[(⊠)], Seonghan Ryu, Kyusong Lee, Yonghee Kim, Sangjun Koo, Jeesoo Bang, Seonyeong Park, and Gary Geunbae Lee

Pohang University of Science and Technology, 77 Cheongam-Ro, Nam-Gu, Pohang, Gyeongbuk, Korea
chasunee@postech.ac.kr

Abstract. We proposed an automatic speech recognition (ASR) error correction method using hybrid word sequence matching and recurrent neural network for dialog system applications. Basically, the ASR errors are corrected by the word sequence matching whereas the remaining OOV (out of vocabulary) errors are corrected by the secondary method which uses a recurrent neural network based syllable prediction. We evaluated our method on a test parallel corpus (Korean) including ASR results and their correct transcriptions. Overall result indicates that the method effectively decreases the word error rate of the ASR results. The proposed method can correct ASR errors only with a text corpus without their speech recognition results, which means that the method is independent to the ASR engine. The method is general and can be applied to any speech based application such as spoken dialog systems.

Keywords: Automatic speech recognition · Error correction · Recurrent neural network

1 Introduction

An automatic speech recognition (ASR) system translates speech input into the correct orthographic form of text. Many applications, such as spoken dialog systems, use ASR as a basic component, and most ASR systems are independently operated. However, ASR system providers occasionally do not provide all necessary components for application development such as the ASR model trainer and the core part of the ASR decoder. Therefore, problems caused by the ASR system should be controlled by tuning the output of ASR, which means that sometimes post-processing is required to correct the ASR errors.

Many previous post-processing methods need parallel corpora which include ASR result texts and their correct transcriptions [1,7,10]. Jeong et al. [7] used a noisy channel model to detect error patterns in the ASR results. The noisy channel model was trained by the parallel corpus. Ringger and Allen [10] proposed a post editing model that uses a noisy channel for error detection and

© Springer International Publishing Switzerland 2015
R. Böck et al. (Eds.): MA3HMI 2014 Workshop, LNAI 8757, pp. 69–77, 2015.
DOI: 10.1007/978-3-319-15557-9_7

error correction with the Viterbi search algorithm to implement the language model. Brandow and Strzalkowski [1] suggested a rule-based method; in a training stage, the method generates a set of correction rules from the ASR results and validates the rules against a generic corpus. In a post-editing stage, the set of rules is used to detect and correct the ASR errors.

However, the parallel corpora are generally hard to obtain and make error correction dependent to specific ASR and acoustic environments. Also, if the ASR system of the application is changed, the error correction model may be ineffective. In this case, the model should be re-constructed from a new parallel corpus which is generated by the changed ASR system. Furthermore, generation of the new parallel corpus is impossible if the parallel corpus includes only texts but not speeches. For this reason, we proposed a word sequence matching based error correction (WSMEC) method which needs only correct transcriptions, that is, normal text corpora [3]. However, the method needs word sequences to correct ASR errors, and the size of the model for WSMEC increases exponentially as the size of the training corpus increases, so to overcome these limitations, we propose a secondary error correction method which uses recurrent neural network (RNN) [8] based syllable prediction.

In this paper, we propose a method for ASR error correction, which is independent from the ASR engine. Unlike the other post-processing methods, the proposed method needs only the corpus that is used for training the application (e.g. dialog system) and that includes only correct sentences. In the following section, we describe our proposed method. In Sect. 3, we show the experimental results and discuss, and finally in Sect. 4, we conclude.

2   Method

Our proposed method (Fig. 1) consists of two parts: ASR error detection and correction. In the error detection part, the system detects errors in the input sentence using multiple methods. In the correction part, words that are identified as errors are replaced or removed. All models that are needed to process the proposed method are constructed from only the text corpus that is used for training the dialog system application.

2.1   ASR Error Detection

ASR error detection is a classification of the word whether it is an error or not. However, this detection cannot be treated as a supervised classification problem because a parallel corpus including ASR results and their transcripts is not provided in our model.

The errors are detected essentially by voting from each of the detection component module that identifies error candidates. The error detection part consists of three components: Part-of-Speech (POS) pattern, word dictionary by POS label, and word co-occurrence. The detection methods are described in [3] and this paper only focuses on error correction method.

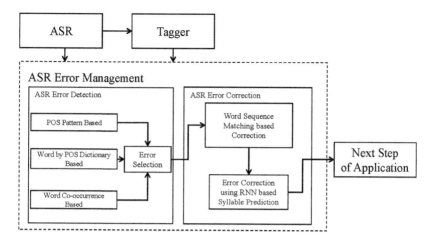

Fig. 1. Architecture of the proposed method

2.2 ASR Error Correction

Basically, ASR errors are corrected by the WSMEC method. The limitation of the WSMEC is that the errors are not corrected without word sequence pattern lexicons, so we consider a secondary method by using an RNN to predict the correct word syllable-by-syllable.

Word Sequence Matching Based Error Correction (WSMEC). WSMEC is based on word sequence patterns and pronunciation sequences. The word sequence pattern is a sequence which consists of 3~5 words (trigram to five-gram) extracted from a sentence in the corpus. For example, the sentence, "This is an example sentence", generates 6 different word sequence patterns: "This is an", "is an example", "an example sentence", "This is an example", "is an example sentence", and "This is an example sentence". To evaluate a word sequence pattern, its pronunciation sequence is useful because even an erroneous sentence can have a similar pronunciation sequence to the correct sentence [2]. For a pronunciation sequence, an in-house grapheme-to-phoneme (G2P) module is used, because we assume that the ASR system provides only output sentences. From the application dialog corpus, the correction model is constructed using word sequence patterns and their pronunciation sequences. The detail word sequence pattern based correction algorithm is described in Fig. 2.

First, the system identifies changeable and unchangeable (fixed) parts. The changeable part includes the detected erroneous words and its neighbor words because the detected erroneous words also have high potential to be recognized incorrectly. Other words are regarded as unchangeable parts (Fig. 3). Then, the system searches for word sequence patterns from the model that match the word sequence pattern in the sentence including the changeable part and its surrounding words. In Fig. 3, the number of applicable parts including a changeable part,

Algorithm 1. WSMEC(I)
Input I - an error-labeled ASR output
Output O - a corrected sentence
1: **Identify** changeable and unchangeable (fixed) parts
2: **For** all changeable parts
1: **Extract** applicable word sequence patterns including a changeable part and its surrounding words
2: **For** all applicable word sequence patterns
1: **Search** matching word sequence pattern from word sequence pattern model
2: **Score** the parts to be replaced in the matched word patterns
3: **Endfor**
4: **Replace** changeable part with the highest scored part
3: **Endfor**
4: **Return** I

Fig. 2. Algorithm of WSMEC

Reference Sentence	This	is	the	sentence	that	will	be	corrected.
ASR Result	This	is	the	sentence	then	will	be	corrected.
Errors					1			
Detected Errors					1			
Unchangeable Parts	1	2	3				4	5
Changeable Parts				1				

Fig. 3. Example of part separation; the numbers mean count of each category.

"sentence then will", is 8 when the maximum surrounding word length option is set to 4, for example: "this is the sentence then will", "is the sentence then will be", "the sentence then will be corrected", "is the sentence then will", "the sentence then will be", "sentence then will be corrected", "the sentence then will", and "sentence then will be".

The matched patterns must satisfy the condition that they do not change the unchangeable parts. Each matched word sequence pattern is evaluated by the similarity between the pronunciation sequence of the pattern and the pronunciation sequence of the word sequence pattern that includes a changeable part and its surrounding words; the evaluation score is added to the part to replace. To evaluate the replacing parts, we use the Levenshtein distance. The equation for a replacing part i is

$$\text{Replacing Part Score } s_i = \sum_{j \in C_i} \frac{\sum_{k \in M_j} (l_j - LevenshteinDistance(t_j, m_k))}{l_j} \tag{1}$$

where C_i is the set of applicable word sequence patterns including a changeable part with a replacing part i; M_j is the set of matched patterns for the applicable word sequence pattern j; l_j is the length of pronunciation sequence for the word sequence pattern j; t_j is the pronunciation sequence of the word sequence pattern j; m_k is the pronunciation sequence of the word sequence pattern k. If the matched patterns are not the same, but the replacing parts of the matched patterns are the same, the parts accumulate a score. After searching and scoring all of the considered surrounding words including the changeable part, the system replaces the changeable part with the replacing part that has the highest score.

Syllable Prediction Recurrent Neural Network Based Error Correction (SPREC). The secondary method uses a syllable prediction based on RNN. Our method continuously predicts syllables at the detected error position, and the length of the prediction depends on the length of the detected error position. For example, if the length of the detected erroneous word is 3, the length of prediction is 2~5. This means that the method generates several words that each have 2~5 syllables. To select a correct word, each generated word replaces detected erroneous word and each revised sentence is evaluated by a word-level likelihood score produced by a language model based on RNN [8]. Then, the sentence with the highest score sentence is selected as the correction. This method is especially complement to the WSMEC because it can handle the errors that are not captured in the word sequence pattern lexicons.

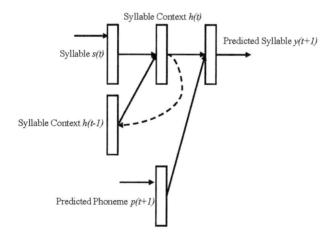

Fig. 4. Network for syllable prediction

The network in our method (Fig. 4) has input layer x, syllable context layer h, predicted phoneme layer p, and output syllable layer y. In position t, the input layer to the network is $x(t)$,the syllable context layer is $h(t)$,the predicted phoneme layer $p(t)$, and the output syllable layer is $y(t)$. Input layer $x(t)$ is formed by concatenating layer $s(t)$ that represents a current syllable with 1-of-N coding and the previous syllable context layer $h(t-1)$. To predict a syllable in position $t+1$, the layers are calculated as

$$x(t) = s(t) + h(t-1) \tag{2}$$

$$h_j(t) = f\left(\sum_i x_i(t)u_{ij}\right) \tag{3}$$

$$y_k(t+1) = g\left(\sum_j h_j(t)v_{kj} + \sum_l p_l(t+1)w_{kl}\right) \tag{4}$$

where f is a sigmoid activation function and g is a softmax function. The predicted phoneme layer p is an additional layer that is included for accurate prediction and is provided in two different ways. First, if the position of the prediction $t+1$, provides the phoneme information, the phoneme layer represents a confused phoneme of syllable of the error position $t+1$, and the layer is calculated from the phoneme confusion matrix [6]. Second, if the position of the prediction $t+1$, cannot provide the phoneme information[1], then the phoneme layer is calculated by the phoneme RNN. The network for the phoneme RNN has input layer x_p, phoneme context layer h_p, and predicted output phoneme layer p. Input layer $x_p(t)$ is formed by concatenating layer $p_c(t)$ which represents a current phoneme with 1-of-N coding and previous phoneme context layer $h_p(t-1)$. To predict phoneme in position $t+1$, the layers are calculated as

$$x_p(t) = p_c(t) + h_p(t-1) \tag{5}$$

$$h_{p_n}(t) = f\left(\sum_m x_{pm}(t)u_{pmn}\right) \tag{6}$$

$$p_o(t+1) = f\left(\sum_n h_{c_n}(t)v_{pno}\right) \tag{7}$$

where f is a sigmoid activation function. Layer p is activated by the sigmoid function, not the softmax function, because this layer is also an input layer to the output syllable layer y, so p should be scaled the same as the syllable context layer h.

---

[1] In some cases, the syllable prediction length is longer than the number of syllables of the detected erroneous word. Then, to predict a syllable, the method must predict a phoneme first.

To train weights u, v and w of the syllable prediction network, a standard back-propagation algorithm is applied with the 1-of-N coding syllable vector to induce that the output syllable layer represents the next syllable. The phoneme RNN is trained independently. For training weights u_p and v_p of the phoneme RNN, a standard back-propagation algorithm is also applied with the 1-of-N coding phoneme vector to induce that output phoneme layer represents the next phoneme.

3   Experiments

We evaluated the performance of the proposed error correction method on Korean texts. For testing, we prepared a parallel corpus ($\sim$6500 sentences). The ASR results were generated by an ASR system whose language model is constructed from an open domain corpus with $\sim$300,000 words and word error rate (WER) of 16.43 %. For the model training of the proposed error detection and correction method, we used a corpus with $\sim$29,000 sentences that do not include the correct sentences of the test corpus.

Table 1. Word error reduction rate of our method

	Word error reduction rate (%)
WSMEC	27.8
SPREC	7.5
WSMEC+SPREC	28.1

Our error correction method reduced WER (Table 1); the combination of WSMEC and SPREC gave the greatest reduction of WER. As a single method, WSMEC was more effective than SPREC to reduce error rate, but WSMEC has the limitations that the method needs word sequence pattern lexicons to correct ASR errors, and that the model size for WSMEC increases exponentially as the number of sentences in the training corpus increases. However, SPREC can correct errors when the word sequence does not exist, and the model size for SPREC depends only on the size of the context layer[2]. Then, we evaluated the word level error reduction rate by each method while varying the word sequence model usage (Table 2). Decreasing the usage of the model for WSMEC increased the word error reduction rate of SPREC. The decrement of the word error reduction rate of WSMEC was higher than the increment rate of SPREC, because WSMEC directly depends on its word sequence pattern data. In situation of dialog applications that use informal sentences, WSMEC has high potential to be unable to correct errors.

---

[2] The number of syllables and phonemes is constant for Korean.

Table 2. Error reduction rate by word sequence pattern model usage

Word sequence model usage (%)	Word error reduction rate by WSMEC (%)	Word error reduction rate by SPREC (%)
100	27.8	0.4
90	25.0	0.5
80	22.2	1.3
70	19.4	1.4
60	16.7	2.7
50	14.0	4.0
40	11.1	4.7
30	8.2	5.4
20	5.6	5.5
10	2.6	7.4
0	0.0	7.5

4   Conclusion & Future Work

In this paper, we proposed a post-processing method for ASR error correction that is independent of the ASR engine. The method operates WSMEC first and SPREC second. WSMEC needs word sequences pattern to correct ASR errors and the size of the model for WSMEC increases exponentially as the size of the training corpus increases, but SPREC overcomes these limitations. We achieved 28.1 % of the error reduction rate for Korean. We also showed each method's word level error reduction rate by varying the word sequence model usage. Furthermore, the error corrected results produced by the proposed method are beneficial for spoken dialog applications by reducing the number of erroneous words that cause unintended system operations.

We are looking for several ways to improved this method. Use of the back-propagation through time algorithm for learning RNNs [9] for syllable prediction and phoneme prediction would provide additional improvements. Additionally, our method trained the syllable prediction network and the phoneme prediction network independently, but the syllable prediction network can back-propagate to the phoneme prediction network; this process might increase the accuracy with which the output layer of the phoneme prediction network represents vector that predict syllable. ASR results combination approaches, such as recogniser output voting error reduction (ROVER) [5] and confusion network combination (CNC) [4], can be applied to combine our WSMEC results and SPREC results. These approaches may improve speech recognition accuracy.

The method is effective for a closed-domain dialog application systems that use an open-domain ASR. For development of ASR applications, they can correct erroneous results using only a corpus for the dialog applications. Additionally, the effect of our method is similar to those of domain adaptation approaches of the language model. Furthermore, because the method is independent of ASR, the method is robust and applicable to any ASR application not only to dialog system application.

Acknowledgements. This work was partly supported by the ICT R&D program of MSIP/IITP [14-824-09-014, Basic Software Research in Human-level Lifelong Machine Learning (Machine Learning Center)] and by the National Research Foundation of Korea (NRF) [NRF-2014R1A2A1A01003041].

References

1. Brandow, R.L., Strzalkowski, T.: Improving speech recognition through text-based linguistic post-processing. US Patent 6,064,957, 16 May 2000
2. Choi, J., Kim, K., Lee, S., Kim, S., Lee, D., Lee, I., Lee, G.G.: Seamless error correction interface for voice word processor. In: 2012 IEEE International Conference on Acoustics, Speech and Signal Processing (ICASSP), pp. 4973–4976. IEEE (2012)
3. Choi, J., Lee, D., Ryu, S., Lee, K., Kim, K., Noh, H., Lee, G.G.: Engine-independent asr error management for dialog systems. In: Intenational Workshop Series on Spoken Dialogue Systems Technology (IWSDS) (2014)
4. Evermann, G., Woodland, P.: Posterior probability decoding, confidence estimation and system combination (2000)
5. Fiscus, J.G.: A post-processing system to yield reduced word error rates: Recognizer output voting error reduction (rover). In: Proceedings of the 1997 IEEE Workshop on Automatic Speech Recognition and Understanding, pp. 347–354. IEEE (1997)
6. Han, D., Choi, K.: A study on error correction using phoneme similarity in post-processing of speech recognition. J. Korea Inst. Intel. Transp. Syst. **6**(3), 77–86 (2007). The Korean Institute of Intelligent Transport Systems (Korean ITS)
7. Jeong, M., Jung, S., Lee, G.G.: Speech recognition error correction using maximum entropy language model. In: Proceedings of INTERSPEECH, pp. 2137–2140 (2004)
8. Mikolov, T., Karafiát, M., Burget, L., Cernocký, J., Khudanpur, S.: Recurrent neural network based language model. In: INTERSPEECH, pp. 1045–1048 (2010)
9. Mikolov, T., Kombrink, S., Burget, L., Cernocky, J., Khudanpur, S.: Extensions of recurrent neural network language model. In: 2011 IEEE International Conference on Acoustics, Speech and Signal Processing (ICASSP), pp. 5528–5531. IEEE (2011)
10. Ringger, E.K., Allen, J.F.: A fertility channel model for post-correction of continuous speech recognition. In: Proceedings of the Fourth International Conference on Spoken Language, 1996. ICSLP 1996, vol. 2, pp. 897–900. IEEE (1996)

Acquisition and Use of Long-Term Memory for Personalized Dialog Systems

Yonghee Kim[⊠], Jeesoo Bang, Junhwi Choi, Seonghan Ryu,
Sangjun Koo, and Gary Geunbae Lee

Department of Computer Science and Engineering, POSTECH,
Pohang, South Korea
{ttti07,jisusl9,chasunee,ryush,giantpanda,
gblee}@postech.ac.kr

Abstract. This study introduces a personalization framework for dialog systems. Our system automatically collects user-related facts (i.e. triples) from user input sentences and stores the facts in one-shot memory. The system also keeps track of changes in user interests. Extracted triples and entities (i.e. NP-chunks) are stored in a personal knowledge base (PKB) and a forgetting model manages their retention (i.e. interest). System responses can be modified by applying user-related facts to the one-shot memory. A relevance score of a system response is proposed to select responses that include high-retention triples and entities, or frequently used responses. We used Movie-Dic corpus to construct a simple dialog system and train PKBs. The retention sum of responses was increased by adopting the PKB, and the number of inappropriate responses was decreased by adopting relevance score. The system gave some personalized responses, while maintaining its performance (i.e. appropriateness of responses).

Keywords: Personalization · Conversational agent · Forgetting model · User model · User interest · User knowledge · Memory

1 Introduction

Spoken dialog interfaces are designed to allow users to communicate with their devices in a human-like way. People show great interest in the human-like reaction of the device. People feel friendly toward the device, and this kind of intimacy indirectly increases user satisfaction in its service. This observations implies that dialog systems can be developed to build rapport with the user by acting as a counselor or a virtual friend. To build rapport with the user, counseling skills such as taking after the user's own words and remembering his/her interests can be used [1]. Dialog systems that adopt these skills might lead to the next generation of dialog systems.

Personalization is not studied much in previous dialog systems. Dialog systems are studied in two ways: task-oriented dialog systems and small talk systems. Task-oriented dialog systems are used to assist in some tasks in specific domains [2]. Recent studies of dialog systems have focused on topics like dialog management strategy [3, 4], multi-domain expansion [5], and incremental processing [6].

© Springer International Publishing Switzerland 2015
R. Böck et al. (Eds.): MA3HMI 2014 Workshop, LNAI 8757, pp. 78–87, 2015.
DOI: 10.1007/978-3-319-15557-9_8

Small-talk systems were developed for the purpose of entertainment. They use simple pattern scripts to respond to various user input sentences [7]. Furthermore, systems like ALICE[1] use pattern rules or instructions to extract user information (i.e. name, hobby) from the user input, and utilize it when they generate responses. However, adding new rules or instructions to these systems is difficult because the rules are interdependent in complex ways. These systems can cover only a restricted range of user information.

Personalization has been researched in the area of information retrieval and recommendation. Personalized search [8, 9] or personalized recommendation systems [10, 11] are popular research topics. Each study has its own domain model, and the user model is designed based on it. However, a domain-specific user model is not suitable for building rapport with users; users want the system to remember all their interests. Moreover, generating a response is a slightly different task from the task of information retrieval and recommendation. The user modeling techniques can be partially adopted to our framework, but their details should be different. Therefore, we propose a new personalization framework for dialog systems to build rapport with users.

Collecting user-related facts is important to develop a personalized system. Our system extracts triples (i.e. (arg_1, rel, arg_2)) from every user input sentence. Extracted triples which include user-related facts (i.e. user-related triples) are picked and stored in one-shot memory. Manually written triple patterns are used to identify user-related triples. They act like pattern rules which are used in previous small talk systems, but triple patterns can be easily added and store user-related facts in structured form.

The system also keeps track of changes in the user's interests, distinguishing long-term interests from short-term conversational topics. We propose a forgetting model to achieve this goal. Knowledge units like triples and entities (i.e. NP-chunks) are extracted from every user input sentence, then stored in a personal knowledge base (PKB). Each knowledge unit in the PKB has retention and strength. The retention represents the user's degree of interest in the knowledge unit. The strength of a knowledge unit prevents the retention from decaying quickly. The forgetting model uses Ebbinghaus' forgetting curve and spacing effect [12]. The retention and strength of a knowledge unit change over time depending on the frequency and aspect of the user's remarks on that knowledge unit. Triples in the one-shot memory have the maximum retention value by default.

System response candidates can be modified by applying user-related triples in the one-shot memory. We extract a triple from a system response candidate and substitute its arg_1 (or arg_2) with the arg_1 (or arg_2) of the user-related triple, when the two triples are similar enough except those arg_1 (or arg_2). We call this technique *triple substitution*. Our system uses this technique to generate personalized responses.

We also propose a relevance score of a system response to select the most appropriate and personalized response. The relevance score uses statistical information of the example database and uses retentions of knowledge units included in the system response. This score puts weight on a response that includes high-retention knowledge units, and also puts weight on general, frequently-used responses. Previous dialog

---

[1] http://www.alicebot.org/.

systems tend to exclude personal information and responses about specific topics from their example database, because the response might not be appropriate for some users. Therefore, responses of the previous systems can be too simple and dull. However, the example database of our system can have various responses owing to its use of the relevance score.

The result of personalization was evaluated using a simple dialog system constructed from the Movie-Dic corpus [13]. Movie-Dic consists of 753 movie scripts, and contains various conversational examples. We extracted (user utterance, system response) pairs from the corpus and stored them in the example database. We also extracted utterances of each movie character to train a PKB. Three dialog systems were constructed in this experiment; a baseline system that uses neither the relevance score nor one-shot memory, a system that uses the relevance score without one-shot memory or PKB, a system that uses the relevance score with one-shot memory and PKB. We prepared 100 test input sentences, and for each system, we got 100 system responses from the 100 inputs. Appropriateness of each system response was evaluated by hand. Adopting the relevance score reduced the number of inappropriate responses. Adopting a PKB increased the number of user-interested responses (i.e. responses which include high-retention triples or entities). We acquired different system responses depending on the system's PKB.

2   Personal Knowledge Manager

We used a triple extractor and a NP-chunker as a knowledge extractor to extract structured knowledge units from user input sentences. Two types of knowledge units are extracted from a sentence; WOE-style triple and entity (i.e. NP-chunk). WOE defines a triple as (arg_1, rel, arg_2), where the args are noun phrases and rel is a textual fragment that indicates the semantic relation between them [14]. All extracted knowledge units are stored in the PKB, and some triples (i.e. user-related triples) are stored in one-shot memory.

2.1   One-Shot Memory

Extracted triples which directly include user-related facts are specially picked and stored in the one-shot memory. Triple patterns are used to identify user-related triples; we define two types of triple patterns: a triple with a subject slot (SBJ, rel, arg) and a triple with an object slot (arg, rel, OBJ). If a triple matches any triple pattern except the slot, the triple is identified as a user-related triple and stored in the one-shot memory. Triple patterns are currently generated manually, and various triple patterns can be used depending on the domain or purpose of the system.

2.2   Personal Knowledge Base

A personal knowledge manager (PKM) uses a forgetting model to manage the PKB. According to Ebbinghaus' forgetting curve, the retention of memory gradually decreases over time, but recharges when it is reviewed [15]. Ebbinghaus also discovered another phenomenon from the forgetting curve, named *the spacing effect*. To remember something solidly, repeated review spaced over a long time span is much more effective than intensive learning within a short period. Once knowledge resides in human memory solidly, it is not easily forgotten. By modeling this forgetting curve, we can distinguish important knowledge units from unimportant ones.

To model Ebbinghaus' forgetting curve, we define retention $r(k)$ and strength $s(k)$ for each knowledge unit k. $r(k)$ represents how much the user is interested in k, and $s(k)$ represents how solidly k resides in the PKB. Whenever k is extracted from the user input sentence, the PKM receives it. If k does not exist in the PKB, the PKM inserts it into the PKB and assigns initial values: $r(k) = 0.8$, $s(k) = 30$. If k already exists in the PKB, the PKM finds targets k' whose $r(k')$ and $s(k')$ should be updated. In the PKB, a target k' is similar to the knowledge unit k, including k itself, when $sim(k', k) > threshold$. We use weighted dice similarity (in Sect. 3, Eq. 4) and set $threshold = 0.8$.[2] The PKM updates $r(k')$ and $s(k')$ on demand; the updating process involves two steps:

- Step 1. Forgetting

$$r(k') \leftarrow r(k') \cdot exp((a(k') - t_c)/s(k'))$$ (1)

- Step 2. Recharging

$$s(k') \leftarrow (1 + sim(k', k) \cdot r(k') \cdot (t_c - a(k))) \cdot s(k')$$ (2)

$$r(k') \leftarrow r(k') + sim(k', k) \cdot \mu \cdot (1 - r(k'))$$ (3)

where t_c is the current time, $a(k')$ is the most recent access time of the target knowledge unit k', and $\mu = 0.8$ is a coefficient.[3]

3 User-Related Fact Applier

System response candidates can be modified by applying user-related triples in the one-shot memory. We extract a triple trp_c from the system response candidates, then convert second-person pronouns of trp_c to first-person pronouns. To find substitutable triples for trp_c from the one-shot memory, two types of queries are generated from trp_c; $(*, rel, arg_2)$ and $(arg_1, rel, *)$, where $*$ is a wildcard character. Matched triples for the queries are retrieved from the one-shot memory. For each matched triples, the noun phrase which is represented as arg_1 (or arg_2) of trp_c in the system response candidate is replaced with the arg_1 (or arg_2) of a matched triple. We call this technique as triple substitution.

---

[2] Knowledge units consist of the same lemmas except their articles and determiners mostly have similarity >0.8.

[3] μ is the same as the initial value of the retention.

For example, when a user-related triple trp_u = (I, like, blue banana) in the one-shot memory is applied to a system response candidate "I know, you like apples.", we extract trp_c = (you, like, apple) from the system response candidate. After the personal pronoun is changed, trp_c = (I, like, apple). Because trp_u matches with trp_c except their arg_2, "apple" in the system response is replaced with "blue banana". The system response is modified to "I know, you like blue bananas". Using this technique, our system can generate personalized response.

4   Relevance Score

Relevance score $rel(s)$ measures the appropriateness of a response s. $rel(s)$ puts weight on responses s which include user-related facts, and also puts weight on general, frequently-used responses. $rel(s)$ is calculated using statistical information about the example database and the retentions of user-related triples in the one-shot memory and knowledge units in the PKB. $rel(s)$ is designed based on the assumption that a general response has many similar responses in the example database. The sum of sentence similarities between a target response s and all responses in the example database $\mathbf{E}$ can measure the generality of s as

$$gen(s) = \sum\nolimits_{(s_u, s_s) \in \mathbf{E}} sim(s, s_s) = \sum\nolimits_{(s_u, s_s) \in \mathbf{E}} \frac{2 \cdot \|s \cap s_s\|}{\|s\| + \|s_s\|} \qquad (4)$$

where $e = (s_u, s_s)$ is an example, s_u is a user utterance, s_s is a system response. s, s_u, s_s are also sentences; a sentence s consists of words w, like $s = \{w_1, w_2, ..., w_n\}$, and s_u, s_s are defined in the same way. We use weighted dice similarity $sim(s, s_s)$ between s and s_s from $\mathbf{E}$. Sentence weight $\|s\|$ on a sentence s is defined as

$$\|s\| = \sum\nolimits_{w \in s} IDF(w) \qquad (5)$$

$$IDF(w) = log(|\mathbf{E}|/cnt(w)) \qquad (6)$$

where $|\mathbf{E}|$ is the total number of examples in $\mathbf{E}$, and $cnt(w)$ is *term frequency* of w in $\mathbf{E}$. Because sentences are short enough and *term frequency* is similar to the number of sentence containing the word, approximated *IDF* works well in dialog systems.

In most cases, the scale of $gen(s)$ can be changed depending on $|\mathbf{E}|$, and we normalize $gen(s)$ to between 0 and 1. We had calculated $gen(s_s)$ for all s_s in $\mathbf{E}$, and learned that $gen(s_s)$ are approximately normally distributed (Fig. 1). To normalize $gen(s)$, we can apply cumulative distribution function F to it.

Relevance score $rel(s)$ of s is derived from $gen(s)$. If w has high retention, the *term frequency* of w should be increased because w is familiar to the user. Therefore, we use $cnt_{usr}(w)$ in $rel(s)$, instead of $cnt(w)$;

$$cnt_{usr}(w) = max(cnt(w), r(w) \cdot MaxCnt) \qquad (7)$$

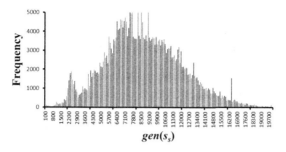

Fig. 1. Distribution of $gen(s_s)$ for all system responses s_s in **E**

where *MaxCnt* is the highest $cnt(w)$ value for all w in **E**. The retention of a word $r(w)$ is defined as

$$r(w) = max(\{r(k)|w \in k, k \in \text{PKB}\}). \tag{8}$$

If w is noun and exists in the one-shot memory, we set $r(w) = 1$. By adopting $cnt_{usr}(w)$,

$$\text{IDF}_{usr}(w) = log(|\mathbf{E}|/cnt_{usr}(w)) \tag{9}$$

$$\|s\|_{usr} = \sum_{w \in s} IDF_{usr}(w) \tag{10}$$

Finally, $rel(s)$ adopts $cnt_{usr}(w)$, $\text{IDF}_{usr}(w)$, $\|s\|_{usr}$, and approximation, then normalizes it.

$$\text{rel}(s) = F\left(\frac{2 \cdot \sum_{w \in s} IDF_{usr}(w) \cdot cnt_{usr}(w)}{\|s\|_{usr} + AvgSentWeight}\right) \tag{11}$$

where

$$AvgSentWeight = \sum_{(s_u, s_s) \in \mathbf{E}} \|s_s\|/|\mathbf{E}| \tag{12}$$

5 Experimental Evaluation

5.1 Experimental Settings

Our simple dialog system is designed to take an input sentence from the user and then to select the most appropriate response from the examples (Fig. 2). User inputs are processed by natural language processing tools like part-of-speech (PoS) tagger, dependency parser and dialog act classifier, and knowledge extractor. Extracted knowledge units are stored in the one-shot memory and the PKB. The PKM manages these knowledge units. The candidate searcher selects some examples from example database. The user-related fact applier modifies the candidate responses by applying user-related triples. The relevance score calculator calculate an example score for each response candidate, then select the one with the highest example score as the most appropriate response. In the baseline system, the example score is $eScore_{base}(u, e) = sim(u, s_u)$, where u is a user input sentence. In the personalized dialog system, the example score is $eScore_{per}(u, e) = r \cdot sim(u, s_s) + (1 - r) \cdot rel(s_s)$ where r is weight on similarity; we set $r = 0.2 + 0.7 \cdot sim(u, s_u)^2$. Note that $eScore_{per}(u, e) = r \cdot sim(u, s_s) + (1 - r) \cdot F(gen(s_s))$, if the system uses neither the one-shot memory nor the PKB.

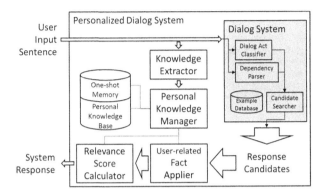

Fig. 2. Personalized dialog system architecture

In principle, we should calculate example scores for all examples given u, but the calculation is too costly because of the large size of **E**. Instead, we select a small set of candidate examples. These candidates can be selected in two ways: by gathering e whose s_u and u share 'common words' or 'rare words', where the commonness or rarity of w are judged by its *term frequency* in **E**. To ignore inflectional changes of w, used PoS-tagged words with their base forms (i.e. likes, liked → like). The process is:

```
INPUT:    u - a user input sentence
OUTPUT:   e* - a set of example candidates
BEGIN
    u' ← {w | w ∈ u, w in E, w is not punctuation}

    Cₛ ← Lem(u')    # Cₛ is a set
    While 1 < size(Cₛ) and size(Rₛ) < 30:
        Rs ←{eᵢ | eᵢ ∈ E, Cₛ ⊂ Lem(sᵤ), da(sᵤ)=da(u)}
        remove the most common word from Cₛ
    Cg ← Lem(u')    # Cg is a set
    While 1 < size(Cg) and size(Rg) < 30:
        Rg ←{eᵢ | eᵢ ∈ E, Cₛ ⊂ Lem(sᵤ), da(sᵤ)=da(u)}
        remove the rarest word from Cg

    Return Rₛ ∪ Rg
END
```

[**Alg. 1**. Candidate Search Algorithm]

Lem(s) = {($base(w)$, $pos(w)$) | $w \in s$} where $base(w)$ is the base form of the word w, $pos(w)$ is the part of speech of the word w and $da(s)$ is the dialog act of the sentence s (e.g. statement, question, greeting).

For system construction, we used our own PoS tagger and dependency parser. The CRF PoS tagger using Ratnaparkhi features [16] shows accuracy of 95.3 % with the same evaluation method of Collins [17]. The dependency parser is based on the MaltParser algorithm [18], which uses the maximum entropy classifier. The dependency parser's unlabeled attachment score is 85.6 %, which is lower than the state-of-the-art [19] but acceptable. The triple extractor is built using core-path patterns which are described in WOEparse [14], but only 360 patterns are used; they were manually extracted from the Movie-Dic corpus, rather than from Wikipedia.

The examples database was constructed using the Movie-Dic corpus. We need sentence pairs as examples, but Movie-Dic consists of dialogs. To convert the dialogs to sentence pairs, we extracted the last sentence of a turn with the first sentence of the next turn, if they have different speakers within the same dialog. OpenNLP sentence boundary detector and some heuristic regular expressions were used to split a turn into sentences. We collected $\sim 360{,}000$ examples without duplications.

We also collected specific movie characters' utterances to train the one-shot memory and the PKB. Ten movie characters from various movies were selected among the characters who had ≥500 utterances. Tick marks were inserted between movie scenes to indicate the flow of the time; the PKM used these marks to update retentions and stabilities of knowledge units. We trained a PKB for each movie character.

Finally, 100 input sentences were picked from unused sentences as test inputs. We excluded sentences that were too specific (e.g. a sentence including a character name) from this set.

We constructed three systems: the *baseline* system that uses $eScore_{base}(u, e)$; the *rel* system that uses $eScore_{per}(u, e)$ without one-shot memory or PKB; and the *relPKB* system that uses $eScore_{per}(u, e)$ with one-shot memory and PKB. The test inputs were given to those three systems, and we received 100 system responses for each system.

Appropriateness of the system responses was evaluated by hand; each response was classified as 'reasonable' or 'nonsense', considering its test input. We also propose retention sum of a response

$$retSum(s_s) = \sum_{w \in s_s} r(w) \tag{13}$$

and also propose using the size

$$\text{pkbSize}(\text{PKB}) = \sum_{k \in PKB} r(k) \tag{14}$$

of a PKB to measure the number of knowledge units and their retention.

5.2   Evaluation Result

Overall appropriateness was not very high, because the example database had many noisy examples. The examples extracted from the Movie-Dic corpus were not refined well to build a dialog system. We just evaluated and compared the responses of the three systems relatively.

By adopting $rel(s)$, the number of 'reasonable' responses was increased significantly. The average $eScore_{base}(u, e)$ of the *baseline* system was 0.62, but the average $eScore_{per}(u, e)$ of the *rel* system was 0.83; low-score responses of the *baseline* system were changed by adopting $rel(s)$, and 87 % of the changed responses had equal or better appropriateness than the responses of the *baseline* system.

By adopting PKBs, appropriateness of the system responses was slightly decreased, but 6.5 % of the system responses were changed from the *rel* system. The ratio of changed responses increased when $pkbSize(PKB)$ was large. Pearson's correlation coefficient between $pkbSize(PKB)$ and the ratio of changed responses was 0.69; they are closely related. The *relPKB* system gave different responses depending on its PKB, and the degree of difference increased with the size of the PKB. The average $retSum(s_s)$ of the *relPKB* system responses was 0.049, while the average $retSum(s_s)$ of the *rel* system responses was 0.029. System responses of the *relPKB* system contained more high-retention knowledge units than the responses of the *rel* system (Fig. 3).

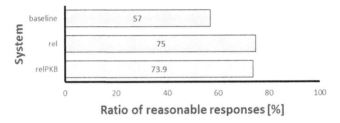

Fig. 3. Ratio of reasonable responses for each system: the *baseline* system used $eScore_{base}(u, e)$; the *rel* system that used $eScore_{per}(u, e)$ without one-shot memory or PKB; the *relPKB* system that used $eScore_{per}(u, e)$ with one-shot memory and a PKB.

6   Conclusion

We proposed a personalization framework for dialog systems to build rapport with the user. Personalized dialog system remembered user-related facts, and applied them to the system response. The system kept track of changes in user interests by adopting Ebbinghaus' forgetting curve. The system mimicked the user's speaking habits or interests by selecting a system response in which the user showed interest. Depending on the user, the system responded in different ways, and the system can develop unique characteristics as the user interacts with it for a long time.

Acknowledgement. This paper was partly supported by ICT R&D program of MSIP/IITP [10044508, Development of Non-Symbolic Approach-based Human-Like Self-Taught Learning Intelligence Technology] and the National Research Foundation of Korea (NRF) grant funded by Korea government (MSIP) [NRF-2014R1A2A1A01003041].

References

1. Leach, M.J.: Rapport: A key to treatment success. Complement. Ther. Clin. Pract. **11**, 262–265 (2005)
2. Zue, V., Seneff, S., Glass, J., Polifroni, J., Pao, C., Hazen, T., Hetherington, L.: JUPITER: A telephone-based conversational interface for weather information. IEEE Trans. Speech Audio Process. **8**, 85–96 (2000)
3. Wei, X., Rudnicky, A.I.: An agenda-based dialog management architecture for spoken language systems. In: Proceedings of IEEE ASRU. Seattle, WA (1999)
4. Young, S.J., Gašić, M., Keizer, S., Mairesse, F., Schatzmann, J., Thomson, B., Yu, K.: The hidden information state model: a practical framework for POMDP-based spoken dialogue management. Comput. Speech Lang. **24**(2), 150–174 (2010)
5. Lee, C., Jung, S., Kim, S., Lee, G.G.: Example-based dialog modeling for practical multi-domain dialog system. Speech Commun. **51**(5), 466–484 (2009)
6. Schlangen, D., Skantze, G.: A general, abstract model of incremental dialogue processing. In: Proceedings of EACL 2009. Athens, Greece (2009)
7. Weizenbaum, J.: ELIZA – A computer program for the study of natural language communication between man and machine. Commun. Assoc. Comput. Mach. **9**, 36–45 (1966)
8. Shen, X., Tan, B., Zhai, C.: Implicit user modeling for personalized search. In: Proceedings of CIKM 2005, pp. 824–831 (2005)
9. Qiu, F., Cho, J.: Automatic identification of user interest for personalized search. In: Proceedings of the 15th International World Wide Web Conference, WWW 2006, pp. 727–736, Edinburgh, Scotland, May 2006
10. Ardissono, L., Gena, C., Torasso, P., Bellifemine, F., Difino, A., Negro, B.: User modeling and recommendation techniques for personalized electronic program guides, Personalized Digital Television: Targeting Programs to Individual Viewers, pp. 3–26. Kluwer (2004)
11. Jiang, Y., Liu, J., Tang, M., Liu, X.F.: An effective web service recommendation method based on personalized collaborative filtering. In: ICWS, pp. 211–218 (2011)
12. Ebbinghaus, H.: Memory: A Contribution to Experimental Psychology. Dover, New York (1885). (Transl. by Ruger, H.A., Bussenius, C.E., 1964)
13. Banchs, R.E.: Movie-DiC: a movie dialogue corpus for research and development. In: Proceedings of the 50th Annual Meeting of the ACL (2012)
14. F. Wu and D. S. Weld, 2010. Open information extraction using Wikipedia. In Proc. of the 48th Annual Meeting of the Association for Computational Linguistics, ACL '10, pp. 118–127, Morristown, NJ, USA
15. Zhou, B., Zhang, B., Liu, Y., Xing, K.: User model evolution algorithm: forgetting and reenergizing user preference. In: Proceedings of the IEEE International Conference on Internet of Things (iThings/CPSCom), pp. 444–447
16. Ratnaparkhi, A.: A maximum entropy part-of-speech tagger. In: Proceedings of the Empirical Methods in Natural Language Processing Conference (1996)
17. Collins, M.: Discriminative training methods for Hidden Markov Models: Theory and experiments with perceptron algorithms. In: EMNLP 2002
18. Nivre, J., Hall, J., Nilsson, J., Chanev, A., Eryigit, G., Kubler, S., Marinov, S., Andmarsi, E.: MaltParser: A language-independent system for data-driven dependency parsing. Natural Lang. Eng. **13**(2), 95–135 (2007)
19. Zhang, Y., Nivre, J.: Transition-based dependency parsing with rich non-local features. In: Proceedings of the 49th Annual Meeting of the Association for Computational Linguistics: Human Language Technologies, pp. 188–193, Portland, Oregon, USA, June 2011

An Automatic Shout Detection System Using Speech Production Features

Vinay Kumar Mittal$^{(\boxtimes)}$ and Bayya Yegnanarayana

International Institute of Information Technology, Hyderabad, India
{vinay.mittal,yegna}@iiit.ac.in

Abstract. Automatic detection of shout in continuous speech is a challenging task. In our recent study, the characteristics of shout and normal speech signals are examined along with the electroglottograph (EGG) signals. The study highlights the changes in the characteristics of both the excitation source and the vocal tract system during production of shout, from those of normal speech. In this paper, we aim to develop an automatic system to detect regions of shout in continuous speech, based upon changes in the production characteristics of shouted speech. Discriminating production features like instantaneous fundamental frequency, strength of excitation, dominant frequency and spectral band energy ratio are extracted from the speech signal. Parameters are derived for the shout decision capturing average level and temporal changes in the features and their pairwise mutual relations. A speaker and language independent prototype automatic shout detection system is developed. Performance evaluation over four databases gave encouraging results.

Keywords: Automatic shout detection system · Dominant frequency · Spectral band energy ratio · Zero-frequency filtering · EGG · Differenced EGG

1 Introduction

Automatic detection of *shout* or *shouted speech* regions in continuous speech has applications in the domains ranging from security, sociology, behaviour studies and health-care access to crime detection [1–5]. Hence, research in acoustic cues to facilitate spotting the shout regions is gaining increased attention in recent times. In this paper, we aim to exploit the changes in the production characteristics of shouted speech as compared to normal speech, for developing an automatic system for detection of shout regions in continuous speech.

Shouted speech consists of linguistic content and voicing in the excitation. The production characteristics of shout, in particular of the excitation source, are likely to deviate from those of normal speech, especially in the regions of voicing. Associated changes also occur in the characteristics of the vocal tract system. In general, changes in the excitation source characteristics are examined by studying the changes in the frequency of vocal fold vibrations, i.e., instantaneous fundamental frequency (F_0) [1,3,4,6]. Changes in the vocal tract system

© Springer International Publishing Switzerland 2015
R. Böck et al. (Eds.): MA3HMI 2014 Workshop, LNAI 8757, pp. 88–98, 2015.
DOI: 10.1007/978-3-319-15557-9_9

characteristics are usually examined in terms of changes in the spectral charac-teristics of speech, such as Mel-frequency cepstral coefficients (MFCCs) [2,5–7].

Studies on the analysis of shout or scream signals mostly used features like F_0, MFCCs and signal energy [1–6]. Features such as formant frequencies, F_0 and signal power were studied in [1,4,6]. Applications of these features included auto-matic speech recognition for shouted speech [1]. The MFCCs, frame energy and auto-correlation based pitch (F_0) features were studied in [2,3,5]. Applications of these features included scream detection using a support vector machine clas-sifier [2]. The MFCCs with weighted linear prediction features were studied for the detection of shout in noisy environment [6]. Spectral tilt and linear predic-tive coding spectrum based features were used in [7], for studying the impact of vocal effort variability on the performance of an isolated word recognizer. The MFCCs and spectral fine structure (F_0 and its harmonics) were used recently, in a Gaussian mixture model based approach for shout detection [8].

In the production of shouted speech, although significant changes take place in the vocal folds vibration [9], but these changes have not been used so far explic-itly for automatic shout detection. In our recent work [9,10], we have studied the excitation source characteristics of shout and normal speech signals along with EGG signals [11]. The closed phase quotient (α) is observed to increase for shout as compared to normal speech [9]. Correspondingly, there are significant changes in the spectral band energy ratio (β) and the standard deviation in low-frequency band spectral energy (σ_{LFSE}). The source features F_0 and strength of excitation (SoE) are also changed [9,10]. Associated changes in the vocal tract system are examined through a feature called *dominant frequency* (F_D) [10]. Features β and σ_{LFSE} are extracted from the speech signal using the Hilbert envelope of double differenced numerator group delay (HNGD) method [9]. The source features F_0 and SoE are extracted using the zero-frequency filtering (ZFF) method [12], and the system feature F_D using linear prediction (LP) analysis [13].

In this paper, we develop an experimental *automatic shout detection system (ASDS)* to detect regions of shout in continuous speech. The system is aimed to be speaker and language independent. The prototype *ASDS* is developed using the production features F_0, SoE, F_D, β and σ_{LFSE}. Since, HNGD is computationally expensive, the features β and σ_{LFSE} are computed using short-time Fourier spectrum. The decision logic uses parameters capturing the degree of deviation in these features for shout, as compared to normal speech. Temporal nature of changes in the features and their pairwise mutual relations are also exploited. The decision of shout/normal is made for each speech segment using the parameters derived from the average values of changes in these features. The major challenge in developing an *ASDS* is the vast variability in shouted/normal speech, that could be speaker, language or application specific. Hence, a rule-based approach is used in the *ASDS*. It collects an ensemble of evidences of shout using multiple parameters. Performance of the prototype *ASDS* is evaluated on four datasets of continuous speech in three languages.

The paper is organized as follows: Sect. 2 discusses changes in the production characteristics of shout, studied from the EGG and speech signals. Methods for extracting features from the speech signal are discussed in Sect. 3. Section 4 describes the parameters derived for shout decision in the *ASDS*. Section 5 discusses the decision logic of the prototype *ASDS*. Performance of the *ASDS* is evaluated in Sect. 6. Section 7 gives a summary and scope of further work.

2   Changes in the Production Characteristics of Shout

Human speech is produced by a time varying excitation of a time varying vocal tract system. The time varying excitation consists mostly a sequence of glottal pulses produced by the periodic opening/closing of vocal folds. In the production of shouted speech, significant changes seem to occur in the proportion of open/closed phase region relative to the period of each glottal cycle, in comparison to that for normal speech [9,10]. Hence, relative durations of open/closed phase regions in each glottal cycle were compared for normal and shouted speech [9]. EGG signal [11] along with a close speaking speech signal for the utterance pairs of same text by same speaker, in both normal and (acted) shout modes (51 such pairs) were used [9]. The comparisons of differenced EGG signals revealed that, *in the case of shout* the duration of glottal cycle period reduces and *the closed phase quotient within each glottal cycle increases* [9,10].

The reduction in the period of the glottal cycle, i.e., the rise in the F_0 gives perception of higher pitch in the case of shout. The larger closed phase quotient in each glottal cycle is related to increased air pressure at the glottis, and also to higher resonance frequencies [9,10]. Correspondingly, there are changes in the features SoE and F_D for shout as compared to normal speech [9,10]. *The spectral energy in the higher frequency band (500–5000 Hz) (E_{HF}) also increases and in the lower frequency band (0–400 Hz) (E_{LF}) reduces for shout*, in comparison to normal speech [9]. These changes are reflected well in the features β and σ_{LFSE}. The feature β ($= \frac{E_{HF}}{E_{LF}}$) increases and σ_{LFSE} decreases for shouted speech, as compared to normal speech [9,10]. Since, using EGG-based features [9] is difficult for any practical application of shout detection, the production features are derived from the speech signal itself, in the *ASDS* developed in this paper.

3   Methods for Feature Extraction

The excitation source features F_0 and SoE are extracted from the speech signal [9,10] using the zero-frequency filtering (ZFF) method [12]. In the ZFF method [12], the differenced signal $x[n]$ is passed through a cascade of two zero-frequency resonators (ZFRs). Each ZFR is an ideal digital filter with a pair of poles at $z = 1$ in the $z-$plane. The effect of passing the differenced signal $x[n]$ through a ZFR ($y[n] = x[n] - \sum_{k=1}^{2} a_k y[n - k]$), where $a_1 = -2$, $a_2 = 1$) is equivalent to the successive integration twice. The trend in the output of a cascade of ZFRs is removed by subtracting the local mean computed over a moving window of size about 1.5 times the average pitch period. The resultant

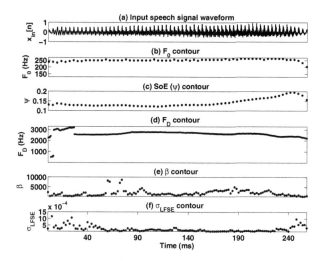

Fig. 1. Illustration of (a) signal waveform and (b) F_0, (c) SoE, (d) F_D, (e) β, (f) σ_{LFSE} contours for a segment of *shouted* speech, for the word "please" in a male voice.

signal is called *zero-frequency filtered (ZFF) signal* [12]. The negative to positive going zero crossings of the ZFF signal correspond to the glottal closure instants (GCIs), called *epochs*. The difference between two successive epochs gives the period (T_0), the inverse of which gives the F_0 [14]. The slope of the ZFF signal around epochs gives the relative *strength of* the impulse-like *excitation (SoE)* around the GCIs. Changes in the F_0 and *SoE* contours for shout in Fig. 1 can be contrasted from those for normal speech in Fig. 2.

In the production of shout, associated changes in the vocal tract resonances occur due to the effect of coupling between the excitation source and the vocal tract system. The effect can be seen better in the feature *dominant frequency* (F_D) of vocal tract system resonances [10], derived using linear prediction (LP) analysis [13]. The location of the highest peak in the LP spectrum, i.e., *dominant* peak *frequency* (F_D), is obtained for a frame of speech signal considered at every sampling instant of time [10]. The F_D value is observed to be significantly higher for shout in comparison to that for normal speech, in the contexts of 5 different English vowels [10]. Changes in the F_D contours for shout from normal speech can be observed in Fig. 1(d) and Fig. 2(d), respectively.

The *spectral band energies* E_{HF} and E_{LF} are computed using the short-time Fourier spectrum, instead of the HNGD method used in [9], for computational convenience. Changes in the features β ($= E_{HF}/E_{LF}$) and σ_{LFSE}, extracted from the speech signal for shouted speech in Fig. 1(e) and (f), can be contrasted from those for normal speech in Fig. 2(e) and (f). It may be noted that the features F_0, SoE, F_D, β and σ_{LFSE} are extracted from the speech signal using computationally efficient methods, so as to achieve less response time of the *ASDS*.

4   Parameters Derived for the Shout Decision

The *degree* of changes in the production features for shout indicates the extent of deviation from normal. The *gradient* of temporal changes in the features computed over successive frames of speech signal, indicates the rapidness of changes in the features for shout in comparison to normal speech. The *nature* of changes relates to the pairwise mutual relations in temporal changes in these features. Parameters capturing all these three aspects (degree, gradient and nature) of changes are exploited for the decision of shouted speech. These parameters are derived in the *ASDS* from the 5 production features F_0, SoE, F_D, β and σ_{LFSE}.

The average values of F_0, F_D, β increase and σ_{LFSE} decreases in the case of shouted speech [9,10]. Hence, the *degree* of changes in the average levels of F_0, F_D, β and σ_{LFSE}, with reference to their respective thresholds are used in the decision of shout candidate for each speech segment. These average values are computed for each speech segment, whereas the reference threshold values are computed either for each block or each utterance of the input speech.

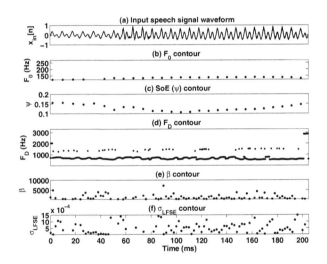

Fig. 2. Illustration of (a) signal waveform and (b) F_0, (c) SoE, (d) F_D, (e) β, (f) σ_{LFSE} contours for a segment of *normal* speech, for the word "please" in a male voice.

It is observed from the F_0, SoE and F_D contours that, in general, changes in these are more rapid for shout than for normal speech. This observation is consistent for F_0 and F_D contours, across speakers and languages. Hence, *gradient* parameters $g_{\Delta F_0}$ and $g_{\Delta F_D}$ are computed for successive frames, capturing temporal changes in F_0 and F_D, respectively. The average $g_{\Delta F_0}$ and $g_{\Delta F_D}$ values above respective thresholds are called *high-gradients* $G_{\Delta F_0}$ and $G_{\Delta F_D}$, respectively.

Temporal *nature* of relative changes in features F_0, SoE and F_D is exploited for discriminating shout from normal speech, using the pairwise relative fall/rise patterns in F_0, SoE and F_D contours. In an illustration shown in Fig. 1, the SoE is increasing for shout when F_0 is (little) decreasing and vice versa (see regions 190–240 ms and 10–40 ms). Likewise, similar/opposite *nature* of fall/rise patterns in F_D contour relative to F_0 and SoE contours (Fig. 1) is also used for the shout decision. Since, units and scales are different for these features, only the directions (signs) of changes in their gradients ($\Delta g_{\Delta F_0}$, $\Delta g_{\Delta SoE}$, $\Delta g_{\Delta F_D}$), i.e., rise/fall patterns, are used.

Total nine parameters derived by capturing the degree, gradient and nature of changes in the features (F_0, SoE, F_D, β and σ_{LFSE}) are used in the decision logic in the *ASDS*. Four parameters capture the *degree* of changes in these features, two capture *gradients* of changes and rest three capture *nature* of pairwise mutual changes in features. For each speech segment, the average values of features F_0, SoE and F_D are used for measuring changes in these over successive segments. This smoothing (averaging) helps in reducing the transient effects of stray fluctuations in these features, and is also computationally convenient.

5   Decision Logic for an Automatic Shout Detection System

In this section, we develop an experimental *ASDS* using the nine parameters derived from five production features. Input speech signal is processed for a block/utterance, each consisting of several segments. Parameters are derived for each segment using average values of changes in the features extracted for successive frames within a segment. Using these parameters, a decision is made for each speech segment - 'whether this segment is a shout region candidate or not?' Major challenge here is the wide range of variations in the features across different speakers, languages and applications. Cultural and other differences related to inherent nature of speakers also may play the role here. For example, some speakers speak normally in soft voice but some may be loud, which makes automatic decision of shout/normal difficult. Hence, a rule-based approach using multiple *decision criteria* $\{d_i\}$ is considered. An ensemble of evidences of shout is collected for each speech segment, using the 9 parameters derived. Higher number of evidences gives higher *confidence* in deciding that segment as shout.

The *decision criteria* d_1, d_2, d_3 and d_4 capture the *degree* of changes in the features F_0, F_D, β and σ_{LFSE}, respectively, using the parameters and thresholds computed from their average values. The decision criteria d_5 to d_9 are related to parameters capturing the *temporal nature of changes* in the features F_0, SoE and F_D. The decision criteria d_5 and d_6 use the parameters and thresholds for the *gradients* ($g_{\Delta F_0}$ and $g_{\Delta F_D}$) of temporal changes in F_0 and F_D contours, respectively. The decision criteria d_7, d_8 and d_9 use parameters capturing the pairwise mutual relations of temporal *nature* (sign) of changes in F_0, SoE and F_D contours. The 3 pairs considered are: F_0 and SoE contours (opposite nature), SoE and F_D (opposite nature), and F_0 and F_D contours (similar nature).

Nine decision criteria $\{d_i\}$ using the production features and parameters are:

$$Ave(F_0) > max(\theta_{F_0}, \phi_{F_0}) \qquad\qquad \Rightarrow d_1 \qquad\qquad (1)$$

$$Ave(F_D) > max(\theta_{F_D}, \phi_{F_D}) \qquad\qquad \Rightarrow d_2 \qquad\qquad (2)$$

$$Ave(\beta) > max(\theta_\beta, \phi_\beta) \qquad\qquad \Rightarrow d_3 \qquad\qquad (3)$$

$$Ave(\sigma_{LFSE}) < min(\theta_\sigma, \phi_\sigma) \qquad\qquad \Rightarrow d_4 \qquad\qquad (4)$$

$$g_{\Delta F_0} > max(\theta_{g_{\Delta F_0}}, \phi_{g_{\Delta F_0}}) \qquad\qquad \Rightarrow d_5, G_{\Delta F_0} \qquad\qquad (5)$$

$$g_{\Delta F_D} > max(\theta_{g_{\Delta F_D}}, \phi_{g_{\Delta F_D}}) \qquad\qquad \Rightarrow d_6, G_{\Delta F_D} \qquad\qquad (6)$$

$$sign(G_{\Delta F_0}) = -sign(g_{\Delta SoE}) \qquad\qquad \Rightarrow d_7 \qquad\qquad (7)$$

$$sign(g_{\Delta SoE}) = -sign(G_{\Delta F_D}) \qquad\qquad \Rightarrow d_8 \qquad\qquad (8)$$

$$sign(G_{\Delta F_0}) = \quad sign(G_{\Delta F_D}) \qquad\qquad \Rightarrow d_9 \qquad\qquad (9)$$

here θ denotes *threshold*, ϕ the *reference*, g the *gradient* and G the *high-gradient*. Here, gradients (g) and high-gradients (G) are derived from the average values of ΔF_0, ΔSoE and ΔF_D computed over successive segments. The reference values (ϕ) for average F_0, F_D, β, σ_{LFSE}, $g_{\Delta F_0}$ and $g_{\Delta F_D}$ are obtained from either the reference speech (if available), or empirically from the average values computed for the block of speech data. The threshold values (θ) are obtained using the average of values computed for multiple frames in a speech block.

The *shout decision* for each speech *segment* is a binary decision, based upon the weighted sum of these nine decision criteria $\{d_i\}$, given as:

$$\sum_i w_i d_i \quad > \quad \Theta_{Shout} \qquad\qquad \Rightarrow \quad Shout! \qquad\qquad (10)$$

where $i = 1, 2, ...9$, w_i are weights and Θ_{Shout} is the *desired confidence level*. The weights $\{w_i\}$ are chosen empirically such that $\sum_i w_i = 1$. A few decision criteria such as d_1, d_2 and d_3 are given relatively higher weights for features F_0, F_D and β, based upon their relative importance observed across speakers/languages. *Confidence scores* are computed for each speech segment, using the weighted sum of decision criteria d_1 to d_9 outputs. Speech segments giving a total confidence score above the desired confidence level are decided as *shout candidate* regions.

Final decision for a shout region is taken at the *utterance* or *block* level of speech data, considering only the contiguous segments of shout candidates. It minimizes the spurious cases of wrong detection, since contiguous segments rather than sporadic shout candidate segments are less likely to be false alarms.

6   Performance Evaluation of the Prototype System

Apart from vast variability in features across speakers, languages and applications, there are few other challenges as well in the automatic detection of shout in continuous speech. First, there is no standard labelled database available in English for utterances in dual (normal/shout) modes. Second, most shout databases used in the past studies are application/language-specific [1,7]. Third, nonavailability of ground truth in the continuous speech data is yet another challenge.

Our aim is to develop an *ASDS* that is speaker, language and application independent. Hence, a heuristics based approach is adopted by capturing the dynamic changes in distinguishing features extracted from the speech signal. Empirical values of thresholds are computed dynamically from the derived parameters, factoring-in the variabilities mentioned. The decision logic also exploits temporal changes in the discriminating features of shouted speech. The *ASDS* uses utterances of same text in dual (normal and shout) modes. Total 51 pairs of utterances by 17 speakers, for 3 texts in English, recorded at Speech and Vision Lab, IIIT, Hyderabad [9], are used. Performance evaluation of the prototype *ASDS* is carried out using 4 test datasets drawn from 4 databases in 3 languages.

Test set 1: Concatenated speech (CS) data consists of 6 concatenated pairs of utterances of same text in normal and shout modes, by 6 speakers. The data consisting of 44 normal/shout regions is drawn from the dual-mode database [9].

Test set 2: Natural continuous speech (NCS) data consists of natural continuous speech files that have shout content interspersed with normal speech. The data consisting of 92 normal/shout regions is drawn from IIIT-H AVE database of 1172 audio-visual clips sourced from movies and TV chat shows [15].

Test set 3: Mixed speech (MixSU) data consists of 184 utterances (98 neutral, 86 shout) by 24 speakers in 3 languages, all interspersed together. The data is drawn from 3 databases: (i) Berlin EMO-DB emotion database in German (535 utterances for 7 emotions) [16], (ii) IIIT-H emotion database in Telugu (171 utterances for 4 emotions) [15], and (iii) IIIT-H AVE database in English (1172 utterances for 19 expressive states) [15]. The test set has 47, 72 and 65 utterances drawn from these databases, respectively, for performance evaluation at *utterance level*.

Test set 4: Mixed speech (MixSB) data is similar to test set 3, but performance evaluation of the *ASDS* on it uses shout decisions taken at *block level* (1 sec each). Test sets 3 and 4, each have data for 645 s duration (591 s voiced).

Ground truth was established by listening to the speech data, by 3 listeners and cross-validating the shout regions. All the test data was labelled manually as shout/normal speech regions. Assumption is made in test data that anger speech is usually associated with presence of shout regions.

The results of performance evaluation of the experimental ASDS over these 4 test sets are summarized in Table 1. The *desired confidence level* (Θ_{Shout}) of 80 % is used. Total number of normal/shout speech regions in each test set, as per ground truth, is given in column (a). The number of speech regions detected correctly as shout/normal speech, the shout regions that missed detection, and the normal speech regions that are detected wrongly as shout are given in columns (b), (c) and (d), respectively. Three performance measures are used: (i) *True detection rate (TDR)* ($= b/a$), (ii) *Missed detection rate (MDR)* ($= c/a$) and (iii) *False alarm rate (FAR)* ($= d/a$). The TDR, MDR and FAR for each test set are given in percentages in columns (e), (f) and (g), respectively. The

Table 1. Results of performance evaluation of shout detection: number of speech regions (a) as per ground truth (GT), (b) detected correctly (TD), (c) (shout) missed detection (MD) and (d) wrongly detected as shouts (WD), and rates of (e) true detection (TDR), (f) missed detection (MDR) and (g) false alarm (FAR). Note:- *CS*: concatenated, *NCS*: natural continuous, *MixS*: mixed speech, *U*: utterance and *B*: block.

Test set #	Data Type	(a) GT	(b) TD	(c) MD	(d) WD	(e)(%) TDR	(f)(%) MDR	(g)(%) FAR
Test set 1	CS	44	40	4	0	90.9	9.1	0
Test set 2	NCS	92	85	6	1	92.4	6.5	1.9
Test set 3	MixSU	184	133	14	37	72.3	7.6	20.1
Test set 4	MixSB	591	471	45	75	79.7	7.6	12.7

block level testing results using shout decisions taken for each 1 s block (test set 4) are better, than for utterance level testing (test set 3). It is because, some utterances in test set 3 are up to 15 s long and *shout* being an unsustainable state often gets interspersed with the normal speech in long utterances, which reduces the decision accuracy.

The shout/normal speech detection performance of 72.3–92.4 % with false alarm rate of 1.9–20.1 %, by using the proposed features, parameters and the decision logic, are better than those reported in [1] as 64.6–92% and 22.6–35.4 %, respectively. This performance is also better than the test results of Gaussian mixture model (GMM) based classifier used in [17] that reported shout detection performance (TDR) of 67.5 %. The results are also comparable with test results of *multiple model framework* approach, using hidden Markov model with support vector machine or GMM classifier in [7], that reported success rate as 63.8–83.3 %, with 5.6–11% miss rate and 11.1–25.3 % error rate (FAR). Actually, the MDR of 6.5–9.1 % and FAR of 1.9–20.1 % achieved with the prototype *ASDS* appear to be better comparatively. Though it is also true that these databases are different.

7   Summary and Conclusion

Automatic detection of shout in continuous speech in real-life practical scenarios is a challenging task. A prototype system to detect regions of shout in continuous speech is proposed in this paper, which exploits changes in the production characteristics of shout with reference to normal speech. Changes in the characteristics of vocal folds vibration and associated changes in the vocal tract system for shout from normal speech are exploited in discriminating these two modes.

The characteristics of the excitation source are captured through F_0 and SoE, and that of the vocal tract system through dominant frequency (F_D). Changes in spectral band energies are captured through ratio β and σ_{LFSE}. Parameters capturing changes in the production features F_0, SoE, F_D, β and σ_{LFSE} are used.

Multiple evidences for the decision of shout are collected for each speech segment, using parameters that capture the extent of deviation in the features and temporal nature of changes in these. Gradients of feature contours are exploited to capture temporal changes in features and pairwise changes in these. Decision for shout for each segment is taken based upon the weighted sum of outcomes of nine decision criteria. The desired confidence level and the contiguity of speech segments are also considered for the *final decision* of shout regions.

Performance of the prototype *ASDS* is evaluated using four test sets drawn from four different databases in three languages. Three performance measures are used: true detection rate, the rate of missed detection of shout and false alarm rate. The performance results are comparable to other reported results and appear to be better. Further, an online shout detection system or an agent can be developed for data from the real-life scenarios or human-machine interaction.

Acknowledgement. This work is partially supported by research collaboration between Speech Vision Laboratory, IIIT, Hyderabad and SAIT, SRI, Bangalore (2010-2013).

References

1. Nanjo, H., Nishiura, T., Kawano, H.: Acoustic-based security system: towards robust understanding of emergency shout. In: Proceedings of the Fifth International Conference on Information Assurance and Security, 2009 (IAS 2009), August 2009, vol. 1, pp. 725–728 (2009)
2. Huang, W., Chiew, T.K., Li, H., Kok, T.S., Biswas, J.: Scream detection for home applications. In: Proceedings of the 5th IEEE Conference on Industrial Electronics and Applications, 2010 (ICIEA 2010), June 2010, pp. 2115–2120 (2010)
3. Rouas, J.L., Louradour, J., Ambellouis, S.: Audio events detection in public transport vehicle. In: Proceedings of the IEEE Intelligent Transportation Systems Conference, 2006 (ITSC 2006), September 2006, 733–738 (2006)
4. Van Hengel, P.W.J., Andringa, T.C.: Verbal aggression detection in complex social environments. In Proceedings of the IEEE Conference on Advanced Video and Signal Based Surveillance, 2007 (AVSS 2007), September 2007, pp. 15–20 (2007)
5. Valenzise, G., Gerosa, L., Tagliasacchi, M., Antonacci, F., Sarti, A.: Scream and gunshot detection and localization for audio-surveillance systems. In: Proceedings of the IEEE Conference on Advanced Video and Signal Based Surveillance, 2007 (AVSS 2007), September 2007, pp. 21–26 (2007)
6. Pohjalainen, J., Alku, P., Kinnunen, T.: Shout detection in noise. In: Proceedings of the IEEE International Conference on Acoustics, Speech and Signal Processing, 2011 (ICASSP 2011), May 2011, pp. 4968–4971 (2011)
7. Zelinka, P., Sigmund, M., Schimmel, J.: Impact of vocal effort variability on automatic speech recognition. Speech Commun. **54**(6), 732–742 (2012)
8. Pohjalainen, J., Raitio, T., Yrttiaho, S., Alku, P.: Detection of shouted speech in noise: human and machine. J. Acoust. Soc. Am. **133**(4), 2377–2389 (2013)
9. Mittal, V.K., Yegnanarayana, B.: Effect of glottal dynamics in the production of shouted speech. J. Acoust. Soc. Am. **133**(5), 3050–3061 (2013)

10. Mittal, V.K., Yegnanarayana, B.: Production features for detection of shouted speech. In: Proceedings of the 10th IEEE CCNC 2013, USA, 11–14 January 2013, pp. 106–111 (2013)

11. Fant, G., Lin, Q., Gobl, C.: Notes on glottal flow interaction. STL-QPSR, KTH, Sweden **26**(2–3), 21–45 (1985)

12. Murty, K.S.R., Yegnanarayana, B.: Epoch extraction from speech signals. IEEE Trans. Audio Speech Lang. Process. **16**(8), 1602–1613 (2008)

13. Makhoul, J.: Linear prediction: a tutorial review. Proc. IEEE **63**, 561–580 (1975)

14. Yegnanarayana, B., Murty, K.S.R.: Event-based instantaneous fundamental frequency estimation from speech signals. IEEE Trans. Audio Speech Lang. Process. **17**(4), 614–624 (2009)

15. Gangamohan, P., Kadiri, S.R., Yegnanarayana, B.: Analysis of emotional speech at subsegmental level. In: Proceedings of International Conference on Spoken Language Processing (INTERSPEECH), Lyon, France, 25-29 August 2013, pp. 1916–1920 (2013)

16. Burkhardt, F., Paeschke, A., Rolfes, M., Sendlmeier, W., Weiss, B.: A database of German emotional speech. In: Proceedings of International Conference on Spoken Language Processing (INTERSPEECH), pp. 1517–1520. ISCA, Lisbon, Portugal, 4–8 September 2005

17. Zhang, C., Hansen, J.H.L.: Analysis and classification of speech mode: whispered through shouted, In: Proceedings of International Conference on Spoken Language Processing (INTERSPEECH), pp. 2289–2292. ISCA, Antwerp, Belgium (2007)

Collecting Data for Automatic Speech Recognition Systems in Dialectal Arabic Using Games with a Purpose

Dayna El-Sakhawy, Slim Abdennadher, and Injy Hamed[✉]

Media Engineering and Technology Faculty, German University in Cairo,
New Cairo, Egypt
dayna.el-sakhawy@student.guc.edu.eg,
{slim.abdennadher,injy.hamed}@guc.edu.eg

Abstract. Building Automatic Speech Recognition (ASR) systems for spoken languages usually suffer from the problem of limited available transcriptions. Automatic Speech Recognition (ASR) systems require large speech corpora that contain speech and their corresponding transcriptions for training acoustic models. In this paper, we target the Egyptian dialectal Arabic. As other spoken languages, it is mainly used for spoken rather than writing purposes. Transcriptions are usually collected manually by experts. However, this proved to be a time-consuming and expensive process. In this paper, we introduce Games With a Purpose as a cheap and fast approach to gather transcriptions for Egyptian dialectal Arabic. Furthermore, Arabic orthographic transcriptions lack diacritizations, which leads to ambiguity. On the other hand, transcriptions written in Arabic Chat Alphabet are widely used, and include the pronunciation effects given by diacritics. In this work, we present the game Maخ̣ameخ̣o (pronouced as makhamekho) that aims at collecting transcriptions in Arabic orthography, as well as in Arabic Chat Alphabet. It also gathers mappings of words from Arabic orthography to Arabic Chat Alphabet.

Keywords: Dialectal Arabic · Speech recognition · Egyptian Arabic dialect · GWAP

1 Introduction

Accurate manual transcriptions of speech is an essential ingredient in constructing reliable *Automatic Speech Recognition* (ASR) systems. Both speech corpora and text corpora are needed to train acoustic and language models respectively. Transcriptions are typically done by trained transcribers or experts. This approach has three drawbacks:

1. It is time-consuming. As transcription is done by few people, it is difficult to gather huge amount of data in limited time. Moreover, in the case of using trained transcribers, it takes hours to days to train the transcribers on the transcription guidelines.

© Springer International Publishing Switzerland 2015
R. Böck et al. (Eds.): MA3HMI 2014 Workshop, LNAI 8757, pp. 99–108, 2015.
DOI: 10.1007/978-3-319-15557-9_10

2. It is expensive. According to [11], the cost of one hour of transcribed speech can reach $100.
3. It may not generalize to the data at hand. This may happen due to the fact that experts or trained transcribers follow strict guidelines. Valid differences in transcriptions would not be present is such gathered transcriptions.

In order to avoid these problems, researchers have shifted their methodology to gather data using crowdsourcing. Crowdsourcing is the act of outsourcing a task that is computationally difficult to be solved not by experts but rather by the crowd. Crowdsourcing has evolved as a successful tool in many fields, such as Natural Language Processing [13] and Machine Translation [14,15]. It has recently received attention in the field of speech recognition. It has proven to be a reliable and inexpensive way to collect speech transcriptions. In [11, 12], speech transcriptions were obtained using Amazon's MTurk[1]. The gathered transcriptions achieved high levels of agreement with the experts' transcriptions. From a cost perspective, the average cost of collecting speech transcriptions using MTurk is one order of magnitude less than that using traditional methods, as stated in [8].

ASR systems for Egyptian dialectal Arabic suffer from the lack of speech corpus. Egyptian Dialectal Arabic is mostly spoken and not written. As the majority of spoken languages, it has limited available text. Moreover, it does not have a standardized way of writing. It may be written with *Arabic Orthography* (AO) or with *Arabic Chat Alphabet* (ACA), known as *Franco-Arabic*, which uses the English Alphabet with numbers to compensate for extra letters. All those factors affect the availability of speech corpora. The first goal of this work is to collect Arabic orthographic transcriptions.

Another problem researchers face with Arabic orthographic transcriptions is the lack of diacritics. Diacritics represent short vowels, nunation, gemination, and silent letters. In [16], this problem was overcome by using ACA for transcriptions rather than AO. This is based on the fact that it usually includes the short vowels that are omitted in AO. Furthermore, it was found that the majority of computer users type faster in ACA than AO according a survey conducted in [16]. The second goal of this work is to collect transcriptions using ACA.

Finally, the third goal of this work is to collect mapping of words written in ACA to their corresponding form in AO. Such a corpus can be used in the task of converting text from ACA to AO and vice versa.

In this work, we present a Game With A Purpose (GWAP) named Maخameخo (pronouced as makhamekho). The aim of the game is threefold:

- Collect transcriptions of Egyptian dialectal Arabic using AO.
- Collect transcriptions of Egyptian dialectal Arabic using ACA.
- Collect mappings of words written in AO to their corresponding form in ACA.

The rest of the paper is organized as follows: In Sect. 2, an overview is given on the Arabic language, crowdsourcing, Games With a Purpose, and previous

---

[1] http://www.mturk.com.

work done in gathering data for ASR systems using crowdsourcing. In Sect. 3, the game Maϳame϶o is introduced. Section 4 presents the evaluation and results. Finally, in Sect. 5, conclusion and future work are provided.

2 Background

2.1 The Arabic Language

The Arabic language is one of the most popular languages in the world. It is the 6th most used language based on number of first language speakers. There are three types of the Arabic language: classical Arabic, modern standard Arabic (MSA), and dialectal Arabic. The classical Arabic is the standard and most formal type of Arabic. MSA is classical Arabic written without diacritic marks. It is the formal written standard language of education across the Arab world and is used in writing, news broadcast, formal speeches, and movies subtitling. However, MSA is not the language used in everyday life and is considered as a second language for all Arabic speakers. Dialectal Arabic is the language used in informal daily communication. Every country has its own dialect, and sometimes there exist different dialects within the same country. Dialectal Arabic is also used in folktales, songs, movies, and TV shows. Egyptian Arabic is the most widely understood dialect among Arabs, due to the interest and acknowledgment the Egyptian films and TV series gain worldwide [5,6].

Transcriptions written in Arabic orthography lack diacritization. Diacritics represent short vowels, nunation, gemination, and silent letters. They greatly affect the pronunciation of words. The absence of diacritization can lead to ambiguity. For example, the word مدرسة has 2 valid meanings: school (madrasa) and teacher (modarresa).

It is common among computer users to use Arabic Chat Alphabet (ACA) in typing dialectal Arabic text. As shown in the example above, the ACA forms of the word مدرسة are written as they are pronounced with no ambiguity in the meaning as in AO. ACA usually includes the pronunciation effects of diacritics. In [16], a survey conducted involving more that 100 Arabic computer users. It was recorded that 86 % of the users stated that they type faster using ACA, 9 % do not feel a difference, and 5 % type Arabic letters slightly faster than ACA. All users asserted that it is almost impossible to type a correct fully diacritized Arabic text.

2.2 Crowdsourcing and Games with a Purpose

Crowd-sourcing is the act of taking a task that is usually performed by experts and addressing it to a large, usually online, group of people. The public users then participate in solving the problems available in the open call. The term is a combination of the words: "crowd" and "outsourcing". The idea is to outsource a task to a crowd of people. Four main factors (known as the 4 Fs) were identified to foster the participation in crowdsourcing: Fame (ex. Wikipedia), Fortune (ex. MTurk), Fun (ex. ESP game [7]) and Fulfilment.

Amazon Mechanical Turk (MTurk) system provides a crowdsourcing platform that allows individuals (referred to as Requesters) to use the human intelligence to perform tasks that computers currently cannot do. The Requesters post tasks known as HITs (Human Intelligence Tasks). Workers (referred to as Turkers) can then choose to solve tasks in return of a predefined monetary value.

Up to 150 billion hours (the equivalent of 17 million years of human effort) are spent playing games every year [17]. This gave rise to Games With A Purpose (GWAP). The idea is to design an interesting game that will get people engaged and knowingly or non-knowingly contribute in the collection of data. Some tasks are very easy, trivial for human brain, yet they're still unsolvable by algorithms such as image recognition and speech recognition. The aim of GWAP is to outsource such tasks to humans in a fun way. The collected data can then be used by machine learning techniques to improve algorithms. Examples of GWAPs are ARTigo [18], Tag-A-Tune [19] and the ESP game [7].

2.3 Automatic Speech Recognition and Games With A Purpose (GWAP)

Automatic Speech Recognition (ASR) is a technology that allows a computer to identify the words that a person speaks into a microphone. The ultimate goal is to have a system that would easily recognize the spoken Arabic alphabets and digits regardless of the environmental noise, gender, and dialect [3,4]. In the past few years, researchers have been investigating the use of crowdsourcing for speech-related tasks. GWAP proved beneficial for 3 tasks: speech transcription, speech acquisition and speech annotation. In this section, an overview on some of the work done in speech transcription using crowdsoucring will be mentioned.

In [10,11], MTurk was used to gather transcriptions. It was found that transcriptions entered by turkers were very accurate. In [9], Rio Akasaka conducted a study that introduced two tasks. The first task was the accent recognition and the second was the transcription. In Task 1, players were asked to identify the native language of a foreign accented speaker of English as quickly as possible out of four randomly generated choices. In Task 2, players were asked to transcribe short recordings that were randomly selected from the ones available through the CSLU-FAE corpus. Comparing the results of both techniques with transcription already provided by other users on the server, Task 1 produced 55.26 % of the accents accurately identified. As for Task 2, 1093 recordings out of the 1257 available were transcribed. In [1] a study was conducted where audio files were collected from the conversation and segmented into five second utterances. Utterances were assigned in batches of ten per HIT and played with a simple flash player with a text box for entry. The results showed that data collected with Mechanical Turk was nearly effective for training speech models, and that the main focus should be on the number of audio files used rather than focusing on quality of the audio files. In [2], Scott Novotney and Chris Callison-Burch conducted a similar study.

In 2011, a survey [20] on the existing literature was provided. It was shown that there is a growing interest in crowdsourcing for speech processing. There were only 4 publications in 2009, the number increased to 14 in 2010, and then 10 papers in early 2011. The majority of the studies were on speech labeling and transcription (59 %), with speech acquisition being the second most frequent topic (27 %, and only 5 studies (14 %) have used crowdsourcing for assessment of speech technology. Most of the studies (57 %) used the AMT for crowdsourcing. 7 of the 37 studies (19 %) involved a game from which researchers could obtain the players judgments for free. Other sources of workers include volunteers (14 %) and other crowdsourcing platforms (11 %). Analysis of the literature also shows homogeneity in the geographical source of papers. Of the 29 papers that were indexed in the survey: 22 are from the United States, 6 are from Europe and only 2 from Asia. As can be seen from the statistics, the work done mainly covered English, with no work covering the Arabic language. Moreover, most of the studies used MTurk while GWAPs were less used.

3   The Game

The aim of this project as mentioned earlier, is to collect Arabic mappings from speech to text written in AO and ACA, as well as mappings from dialectal Arabic words written in traditional Arabic orthography to their corresponding form in ACA. This paper presents a GWAP named Ma7ame7o (pronounced as makhamekho) that helps transcribe as many audio files as possible to Franco-Arabic and Arabic. In this section, a description of the game will be given.

Ma7ame7o is a single-player game where the player hears an audio-file and is required to give the corresponding Franco and Arabic transcription. Audio-files used are of 5–7 s and there is no limit to the number of times the player can hear the audio-file. The audio files where chosen to have a few seconds' duration to avoid short-term memory saturation. The game page shows the audio-file, text-areas to enter player's transcriptions and top 2 transcriptions to choose from are displayed. It also shows the label for the player's current skill. The player listens to the audio and needs to transcribe what he heard either by entering his own transcriptions in the text-areas or choosing one of the top transcriptions displayed as shown in Fig. 1. If the user chooses to enter his own transcription, he/she must make sure that the number of words in Franco is equal to that in Arabic. The Top 2 transcriptions are the highest transcriptions entered by other users for this audio.

3.1   Incentives

In order to make the game more creative & challenging, the following incentives were added to the game:

Fig. 1. Game page

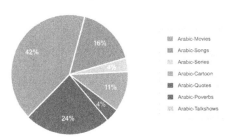

Fig. 2. Survey results

Categories

In order to accomadate for different users' interest, the game includes different categories to increase the variety of the game and make it more entertaining. The categories were obtained by conducting a survey in which a pool of people were asked to choose their favorite categories from a pool of predefined categories. The provided choices were: Arabic-Movies, Arabic-Series, Arabic-Cartoon, Famous Arabic-Quotes, Arabic-Songs, Arabic-Proverbs and Arabic-TalkShows. As shown in Fig. 2, Out of fifty five people who took the survey, twenty three chose Arabic-Movies, thirteen chose Arabic-proverbs, while nine chose Arabic-songs, six chose Arabic-cartoons and finally only 2 chose Famous Arabic-Quotes and Arabic-series. The top 4 categories were chosen for the game (Arabic-Movies, Arabic-Proverbs, Arabic-Songs and Arabic-Cartoon).

Score

To make the game more engaging and motivate the user to enter correct transcriptions, a score is given to the players. Score is calculated as follows:
- If the user chooses the transcription with highest verification 15 points are added to the score.
- If the user chooses the second highest transcription 10 points are added to the score.

- If the user enters a new transcription in the text area 5 points are added. Furthermore, 5 points are added every time a player chooses this transcription from the list of the top 2 transcriptions.

Highest Verification is calculated by counting the number of repeated Arabic and Franco transcription for a given audio-file. Accourdingly the most repeated Arabic and Franco transcription is considered to be the transcription with the first **highest Verfication**. The second most repeated Arabic and Franco transcription is considered to be the transcription with the second **highest Verfication**.

Skill

The player skill is levelled up according to his/her score.

- Beginner: At the start of the game.
- Amateur: Score more than 100 points.
- Semi-pro: Score more than 200 points.
- Expert: Score more than 500 points.
- Pro: Score more than 1000 points.

Hall Of Fame

The Hall of Fame page will include the player of the day, top 6 monthly ranking and top 3 scores in the game. Finally levelling the player's skill after scoring some points will make the players eager to score as many points as possible to level up.

3.2 Collected Data

In this game, two types of data are collected:

- Transcriptions using AO and ACA. These are gathered from users by either entering them directly into the text areas or choosing from the top 2 transcriptions previously given to the audio file. This is done for each of AO and ACA.
- Mappings of AO-ACA words. This is done by making sure that the number of words used in transcription are equal for both cases, AO and ACA. This gives a one-to-one mapping of words. For example, the word الكتاب will be written in one text area in ACA as "Al Kitab".

3.3 Game Framework

The Framework used is **Play Framework 2.2.0**. Play framework is a framework that is inspired from Ruby on rails and Django and follows the model-view-controller (MVC) architectural pattern. It uses both Java to design the backend part and HTML to design the frontend. Play Framework provides an object-relational mapping product written in Java called EBean. This Object-relational mapping along with RawSQL were used to design relationship between the models and create the game's database.

4   Evaluation and Results

The evaluation for Maȝameȝo was held in a duration of two weeks. In this period, 118 users played the game, with a total of 1121 game rounds. 120 audio files were transcribed with 1121 Arabic orthographic transcriptions and 1121 transcriptions in the Arabic Chat Alphabet.

It was observed that in the case of AO, each audio file was transcribed with 1–2 unique transcriptions. However, in the case of ACA, the number was much higher. Out of the 1121 transcriptions, there are 602 unique transcriptions for the 120 audio files. This gives an average of nearly 5 unique transcriptions for each audio file. This observation could have two possible interpretations:

– There is more variation in typing in the case of ACA than AO.
– Users might be more used to typing in ACA than AO. Therefore, they tend to choose from the top 2 transcriptions in the case of AO. This assumption could be valid for the age group of 20–25. However, in the age group of 40–50, users are usually familiar with typing in AO. Therefore, this interpretation is less likely.

It was also observed that the chosen category depends on the age group. For the age group 20–25, users mostly chose songs and films. For the age group 40–50, the proverbs category was the most popular.

Validating the Correctness of the Gathered Transcriptions. The ability of Maȝameȝo to collect the correct transcriptions was evaluated on a small sample of the audio files. Some of the participants were asked to provide transcriptions for 5 audio files. The audio files were selected for each participant to be in different categories than those chosen in the game. The transcription provided by each participant for an audio file was checked whether it was gathered from the game or not. All the transcriptions were found to be collected through the game. This shows that the game is capable of collecting correct transcriptions. Moreover, the data collected includes the different variations in typing, which is one of the advantages of using the crowd rather than experts to collect transcriptions.

Validating the Correctness of the Gathered Mappings. The 8 audio files receiving the highest number of different ACA transcriptions were investigated in this evaluation. For each file, the mapping with the most popular ACA transcription was validated. Fifty users were asked to rate each of the 8 mappings on a four-scale. They were asked to rate the mapping of the provided ACA with the corresponding AO. On average, 53.825 % of the ratings were selected to be *strongly agree*, 44.625 % were *agree*, and only 1.5 % of the ratings were given *fair*. These figures show that the game is able to gather mappings of ACA to AO transcriptions. This is only a preliminary evaluation. Further testing should be done on the rest of the mappings gathered. Testing should also be done on word-to-word mappings.

Questionnaire. In order to asses the players' satisfaction with the game, 50 participants filled in a questionnaire. Participants were asked to use a four-scale (strongly agree, agree, disagree and strongly disagree) to answer the following 2 questions:

1. Did you find the game interesting?
2. The game is easy to play?

The participants' feedback on the these 2 questions is shown in Fig. 3. All participants stated they would play the game again.

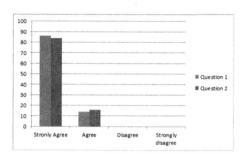

Fig. 3. Participants' feedback on Questions 1 (Did you find the game interesting?) and Question 2 (The game is easy to play?)

5   Conclusion

Automatic Speech Recognition systems for Egyptian Dialectal Arabic suffer from the lack of existing speech corpora needed for training. Moreover, most available transcriptions do not include short vowels and diacritics that reflect differences in pronunciation which leads to ambiguity. Transcriptions in Arabic Chat Alphabet (ACA) include the pronunciation effects given by diacritics. Maڕameڕo was proposed as a Game With a Purpose that aims at collecting: (1) transcriptions in AO, (2) transcriptions in ACA and (3) Mappings of words from AO to ACA. The game allows people to transcribe many audio files by playing an interesting and challenging game. Results show that the game succeeded in collecting many correct transcriptions as well as mappings from AO to ACA. Participants found the game interesting and easy to play and confirmed that they would play it again. Further evaluations should be done to accurately assess the correctness of the gathered data.

References

1. Suendermann, D., Liscombe, J., Pieraccini, R.: How to drink from a fire hose: one person can annoscribe 693 thousand utterances in one month (2010)
2. Novotney, S., Callison-Burch, C.: Cheap, automatic speech recognition with non-expert transcription, fast and good enough (2009)

3. Delendik, Y.: What is Automatic Speech Recognition? June 2009
4. Furui, S.: Automatic speech recognition and its application to information extraction (2001)
5. Verguria, D., Kirchhoff, K.: Automatic diacritization of arabic for acoustic modeling in speech recognition (2014)
6. Macmillan, P.: Sacred Language, Ordinary People: Dilemmas of Culture and Politics in Egypt. Palgrave Macmillan, New York (2003)
7. von Ahn, L., Dabbish, L.: Designing games with a purpose (2008). https://www.cs.cmu.edu/~biglou/GWAP_CACM.pdf
8. Parent, G., Eskenazi, M.: Toward better crowdsourced transcription: transcription of a year of the let's go bus information system data (2010)
9. Akasaka, R.: Foreign accented speech transcription and accent recognition using a game-based approach (2009)
10. Marge, M.R., Satanjeev, B., Rudnicky, A.I.: Using the amazon mechanical turk to transcribe and annotate meeting speech for extractive summarization (2010)
11. Marge, M.R., Satanjeev, B., Rudnicky, A.I.: Using the amazon mechanical turk for transcription of spoken language (2010)
12. Evanini, K., Higgins, D., Zechner, K.: Using amazon mechanical turk for transcription of non-native speech (2010)
13. Snow, R., O'Connor, B., Jurafsky, D., Ng, A.Y.: Cheap and fast - but is it good? Evaluating non-expert annotations for natural language tasks. In: Proceedings of EMNLP, vol. 1, pp. 254–263 (2008)
14. Denkowski, M., Al-Haj, H., Lavie, A.: Turker-assisted paraphrasing for English-Arabic machine translation. In: Proceedings of NAACL-HLT, pp. 66–70 (2010)
15. Ambati, V., Vogel, S.: Can crowds build parallel corpora for machine translation systems? In: Proceedings of NAACL-HLT, pp. 62–65 (2010)
16. Elmahdy, M., Gruhn, R., Abdennadher, S., Minker, W.: Rapid phonetic transcription using everyday life natural Chat Alphabet orthography for dialectal Arabic speech recognition. In: 2011 IEEE International Conference on Acoustics, Speech and Signal Processing (ICASSP), pp. 4936, 4939, 22–27 May 2011
17. McGonigal, J.: Reality is Broken: Why Games Make Us Better and How they Can Change the World. Penguin Press, New York (2011)
18. Wieser, C., et al.: ARTigo: Building an artwork search engine with games and higher-order latent semantic analysis. In: First AAAI Conference on Human Computation and Crowdsourcing (2013)
19. Law, L.M.: TagATune: A game for music and sound annotation. In: ISMIR, vol. 3 (2007)
20. Parent, G., Eskenazi, M.: Speaking to the crowd: looking at past achievements in using crowdsourcing for speech and predicting future challenges. In: INTERSPEECH (2011)

Author Index

Printed in the United States
By Bookmasters